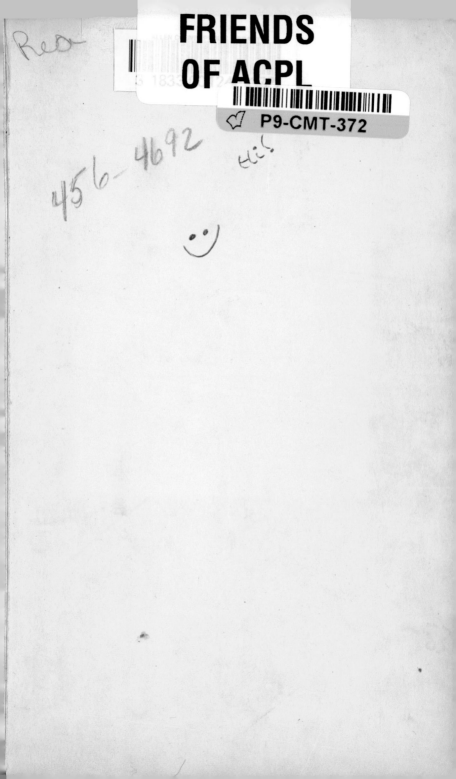

Jean-Paul Sartre

THE EXISTENTIALIST ETHIC

Jean-Paul Sartre

The Existentialist Ethic

by NORMAN N. GREENE

THE UNIVERSITY OF MICHIGAN PRESS

Ann Arbor

Copyright © by The University of Michigan 1960
Published in the United States of America by
The University of Michigan Press and simultaneously
in Toronto, Canada, by Ambassador Books Limited
Library of Congress Catalog Card No. 60-9975
Designed by Stuart Ross
Manufactured in the United States of America by
Vail-Ballou Press, Inc., Binghamton, N.Y.

PREFACE

Jean-Paul Sartre is a contemporary, not only because he is relatively young and still a productive writer, but also because his thought is primarily concerned with the problems of modern man. As a leading representative of existentialism, the newest tradition in western philosophy, he attempts to come to terms with the human situation within the context of the intellectual climate of the middle of the twentieth century. The element of novelty in his thought has complicated understanding of his point of view for those who take their frame of reference from one of the older systems, such as Catholicism, liberalism, or Marxism. At the same time, Sartre has something in common with the older ideologies insofar as he attempts to supply a systematic framework for the understanding of man and society as they in fact are and also as they should be. The minimum value of Sartre's writings is that of any coherent theory of the nature of man. Such an enterprise inevitably cuts across the boundaries of the specialized disciplines into which the study of man is now divided, and cannot therefore be adequately understood in terms of any one of them. An appreciation of Sartre's doctrine requires some familiarity with the achievements of the social sciences in the fields of psychoanalysis, psychology, sociology, anthropology, and political science as well as with current trends in philosophy. That such breadth of knowledge is today rare, and that those who are most competent as students of man are also highly specialized, should not be allowed to obscure the importance of a theory which undertakes to explore man as an irreducible totality rather than as a collection of unrelated behaviors. An understanding of the whole man and his relation to society has been and remains the necessary foundation of every view as to what is good for man as an individual and as a member of society.

The ideologies which Sartre criticizes offer both a description of social reality and a definition of the proper relationship between the individual and society. They are philosophies which prescribe attitudes and actions for individuals, and thus help to determine how men live. Sartre's criticisms of liberalism, Marxism, and Catholicism are significant both as an assessment of the contemporary meaning of these ideologies, and as an indication of the probable influence of existentialism on our conception of man. Sartre is foremost among existentialists in the importance which he gives to the problem of communication, and has not hesitated before the task of exposing the conclusions to which he is led by his philosophy to the general public. It is his belief that what men think is vital not only to the conduct of their personal lives but also to the righting of social evils.

We feel that we may be excused for not taking part in the controversy over whether or not Sartre's ontology is scandalous, his view of humanity depressing, and his political influence in France unfortunate. The task of dispelling some of the confusion about what Sartre really means is formidable enough in itself. The violent emotions aroused by Sartre's writings testify to the reality of the problems to which he has devoted his attention. In order to reject Sartre's position it would seem to be at least necessary to first understand it.

CONTENTS

CONTENTS

Sartre and Existentialism

The editor of a recent anthology of twentieth-century philosophy describes the existentialists as hedgehogs of contemporary philosophy. He uses the term, taken from Isaiah Berlin's *The Hedgehog and the Fox,* to indicate the difference between existentialism and the dominant philosophical movements of the Anglo-Saxon countries; the existentialists are interested in *one big thing*—"philosophies as maps of the universe or as total insights into man's desperate, anxious, forlorn existence," [1] while the analytic philosophers are interested in *one* or *many little things,* such as the methods of science or the meaning of words. The willingness of the existentialists to address themselves to problems ignored by other philosophical schools has had something to do with their considerable popular influence in Europe, where they dominate the philosophic world outside of the two orthodoxies of Catholicism and Marxism. And like the two older systems, existentialism has become an article for export.

Jean-Paul Sartre, the most widely known existentialist philosopher, was born in Paris in 1905. After his father died, he lived with his mother and her parents. His maternal grandfather, an Alsatian named Schweitzer, was the inventor of the Berlitz method of teaching languages, and it is through this side of the family that he is related to his famous cousin, the philosopher Albert Schweitzer. His religious background, like that of André Gide, was part Catholic and part Protestant. Although his health was delicate, he did well in school and gave evidence of a lively imagination. When he was eleven, his mother remarried, and they went to live with his stepfather in the small coastal city of La Rochelle. In his studies there he showed a strong distaste for mathematics, and graduated from high school with a rank of only slightly above average. He continued his studies at Paris in the field of philosophy; after failing his examinations for a degree on his first try, he took them again the following year and passed with the highest grade in his class. After graduation he served for sixteen months in the army, pursued his studies in Germany under, among others, Husserl, and taught high school in Le Havre and then Paris. Le Havre served as the model for Bouville, the town in which the greater part of his novel *Nausea* takes place. In 1939 he again entered military service, was captured by the Germans, and spent some time in a prisoner-of-war camp, from which he was released because of bad health to return to Paris where he remained until the end of the war.

Prior to World War II Sartre published studies in psychological theory and began his activities in the fields of literary criticism and creative writing. The novel *Nausea,* published in 1938, was very popular with his contemporaries but was too controversial to receive any literary prizes at the time. Much of Sartre's philosophy is implicit in this work, and the scandal which it created was not because of any supposedly pornographic characteristics but rather because of the disquieting ideas which it embodied. The fact that much of Sartre's philosophy was developed in these early writings—preceding by several years his major philosophical work *Being and Nothingness* (Paris, 1943)—indicates that the genesis of his philosophy is not to be found in the events of the War, as some have supposed. The vogue of existentialism in postwar Paris and the extent of the reputation which Sartre had acquired by 1946 as a spokesman for the new philosophy may well have been due in part to the War. However, since even in France the audience for works of technical philosophy is restricted, the most important factor in bringing Sartre to the attention of the public at large was his success as a playwright. Both *No Exit* and *The Flies* were first produced under the German occupation, and the latter was more or less widely understood in France to portray the drama of the French Resistance, which had been rendered acceptable to the German authorities by being transposed into the form of a Greek myth.

At any rate, and partly because of its very novelty, the term existentialism entered the daily vocabulary of people who lacked any knowledge of or inclination toward philosophy. In the United States existentialism was described as the esoteric creed of Parisian bohemians, and became associated with jazz, café singers, and pony tails. The connotations of the word were such that some philosophers, as for example Heidegger, hastened to deny that they were existentialists. Sartre, while critical of the misuse of the term, did not disown it. Through no fault of his own, he was identified as the high priest of the movement; most of his publicity was sharply critical, which of course made him the idol of rebellious youth.

This period is now ancient history, but must be evoked because of the effect which it has had on the attitudes of even relatively informed commentators toward Sartre. Public opinion formed by articles in *Life* magazine came to regard Sartre and existentialism with the mingled attitudes of fascination and contempt which are the standard responses to such marginal social phenomena, most recently represented by the Beatniks. Consequently, now that existentialism has begun to be respectable, and even taught in philosophy courses at universities, some commentators go so far as to dissociate Sartre from existentialism or to indicate that he is a minor and unrepresentative figure in the movement.

Insofar as this tendency has made people aware that Sartre is not the only existentialist, something has been gained. Existentialism has exponents in all important European countries, with the possible exception of England, and among its contemporary representatives the Germans Heidegger and Jaspers and the Frenchman Gabriel Marcel are as well known as Sartre to philosophers. Although the roots of existentialism have been traced back as far as Socrates, the Stoics, St. Augustine, and Pascal, the founder of modern existentialism is generally agreed to be Søren Kierkegaard (1813–55). He combined his philosophic abilities with considerable literary talent, but the fact that he wrote in Danish—and was not a very popular figure in the Denmark of his time—restricted the spread of his ideas. The first major language into which his words were translated was German, about the end of the last century, and his ideas began to attract attention in Germany in the period after the First World War. He was translated into French during the twenties and thirties, while in the United States English editions of his books were available only after 1940. In each of these countries, however, some Kierkegaardian themes had already made their appearance. In Germany Friedrich Nietzsche, in France Henri Bergson, and in the United States William James advocated views which are in some respects congruent with those of modern existentialists.

All of these men attacked Hegel and his Universal Philosophy, which Kierkegaard referred to as "the System." But what is more significant is their reason for rejecting the Hegelian synthesis: it was a deep antagonism toward any explanation of the world in terms of abstract reason and a strong bias toward the claims of the existing individual. The term "existing individual" as used by Kierkegaard and his existentialist followers refers not so much to a universal concept of human nature as to a factual entity: a particular individual engaged in the task of living his life. The existing individual is the starting point of existentialist philosophers, and it is his problems that engage their energy. Not that they, in the Hegelian style, erect a system into which he can fit comfortably; instead, they undertake a psychologically oriented study of his inner life.

Kierkegaard criticized Hegel's system as a logical construct with no roots in or meaning for Hegel as a concrete individual existent:

It is from this side, in the first instance, that objection must be made to modern philosophy; not that it has a mistaken presupposition, but that it has a comical presupposition, occasioned by its having forgotten, in a sort of world-historical absent-mindedness, what it means to be a human being. Not indeed, what it means to be a human being in general; for this is the sort of thing one might even induce a speculative philosopher to agree to; but what it means that you and I and he are human beings, each one for-himself.[2]

It is Kierkegaard's contention that one who knows what it means to be an individual human being will realize thought by itself to be incapable of revealing reality. Man gains access to reality not by speculation but by experience, and Hegel by attempting to know the world without first knowing himself as the subject who experiences the world is a comic figure. The objection has often been made to Kierkegaard's view that, if attention is to be directed only toward the peculiar experiences of particular individuals, communication, let alone philosophy, is impossible. This would only be true, however, if a prior assumption is made that the experiences of each individual are entirely unique. While there may be some truth in such an assumption, it certainly is not self-evident. Kierkegaard believed that a philosophy which could define in advance what men have in common was itself impossible. "Now, while the existing individual undoubtedly comes after the preceding six thousand years, if we assume that he spends his life in arriving at a systematic understanding of these, the strangely ironical consequence would follow, that he could have no understanding of himself in his existence, because he had no existence, and thus had nothing which required to be understood afterwards." [3]

In recent times Kierkegaard's *parti pris* in favor of the existing individual has received support from a growing recognition of the great diversity of human behavior and institutions which has come from sociological and anthropological research. This diversity has made the risks of proceeding from a general definition of man to the life of an individual seem too great. Many have drawn the conclusion of Möllberg in Malraux's novel: "If mental structures disappear forever like the Plesiosaurus, if civilizations follow each other only to hurl man into the endless pit of nothingness, if the human adventure maintains itself only at the price of an implacable metamorphosis, it matters little that men transmit for a few centuries their concepts and their techniques: for man is an accident, and, essentially, the world is made of forgetfulness." [4] If there exists a fact which can serve as the foundation for a notion of man, it cannot be found in the discontinuous periods of history or by comparison of incomparable societies. The existentialists have attempted to find it in the inner life of the existing individual. They have attempted to find out what man is, starting from the fact that he is, that he exists; hence the name "existentialism."

It is possible to describe briefly some of the basic themes that occur and recur in the works of existentialist writers which will indicate what Sartre owes to the existentialist tradition. All of the philosophers of existence follow Kierkegaard in asserting the primacy of the existing individual. This involves much more than simply a choice of subject matter; although it would not be an arbitrary choice, since man could well be considered the most important subject matter for man. But, these philosophers maintain, knowledge of the problem of "existence" is not merely one possible branch of knowledge; it is rather the essential basis of all knowledge. They feel with Kant that philosophy must begin with an analysis of the knowing subject, of what it means to be a human being.

Kant, however, undertook an analysis of reason, which he took to be man's instrument for knowing. The existentialists regard reason as only one aspect of human existence and try to go behind it, so to speak, and grasp existence itself. Reason is a tool which can be effective only so long as it is used for the purposes to which it is adapted. If reason is used indiscriminately as the key to all problems it falsifies reality and masks the factual conditions of existence. This position constitutes a radical break with idealist philosophy, by rejecting the Hegelian view that the rational is the real. It carries one step further the evaluation which, in Hegel, led to the substitution of the dialectic for traditional logic; the movement from a tradition which finds in contemplation the key to ultimate reality, and identifies the laws of logic with the laws of reality, to the view that reason distorts reality and is an untrustworthy path to understanding.

As a result of this attitude toward reason existentialist philosophy necessarily regards the fact of individual existence as irrational. It is only after man comes upon the scene, after he exists, that he can ascribe reasons, and therefore existence itself is beyond explanation. The rationally determined characteristics of something have traditionally been termed its essence, so we have the formula which is frequently employed as a definition of existentialism: existence, at least in man, is prior to essence. Associated with this view is the conclusion that there is no providence or rationally intelligible pattern which determine man's future and explain his past. Similarly, there is no rationally intelligible human type which each individual is obligated to realize. This conclusion separates the existentialist not only from idealism but from much of traditional European ethics.

So far, the description of the existentialist position has been primarily in terms of what it rejects. The consequences of disallowing providence are first, that each individual is called upon to invent "man," and secondly that history, in the strictest sense, is made by man. One of the primary characteristics of human life is futurition, or constant striving toward a projected goal which is never fully attained. This concept differs from that of development because it involves neither a set of possibilities given in advance to be realized or progress toward a determined goal. The distance forever between the individual and his goal thrusts upon him the necessity of choice, and for these free choices the individual himself is responsible. Individual responsibility means in this context that there is no authority for the rightness of a decision which can serve as its justification, and that the individual must bear the weight of his freedom in solitude.

Such freedom is, apparently, difficult to bear, and one of the constant themes of existentialist writers is the inevitability of suffering and anguish. Man must feel that he has acted rightly and yet has no reliable guide to right action, so that regardless of exterior circumstances life is a constant trial. Recognition of the inevitability and human importance of suffering is considered a mark of the superior man, who faces life instead of fleeing from it. For the possibility of flight is another existentialist theme. Escape from freedom, while not strictly possible because of its central role in human reality, is a constant temptation. It takes the form of what might be termed a flight from self-consciousness into an illusory security. Hegel found security in his system, which assigned to each individual his place and duty within the perspectives of world history. Other less exalted "systems," in which the routine of daily life holds a preeminent position, are the appropriate place of refuge for less philosophic individuals. Instead of flight the existentialists advise affirmation of life and reconciliation with oneself.

Such a reconciliation is not, for the existentialist, a private matter. Contemplation as an ideal would seem to encourage withdrawal into oneself, away from the world and society. Experience, which existentialism substitutes for contemplation as the source of knowledge, turns the individual toward the world and other people. This is the

theme of engagement; man finds himself engaged in a
situation, and in spite of the fact that he has not chosen
this situation must engage himself freely in it. He must
choose to live his situation because it is beyond his power
to separate himself from it. A final theme, closely related
to that of engagement, is action. Self-affirmation in a
situation where one is involved with other people requires action, and the history of man is that of his *vita
activa*.

It is of course impossible to do justice to the point of
view of existentialism in such a brief summary. Nevertheless, this discussion should indicate what Sartre owes
to other existentialists; as Emmanuel Mounier has noted,
the essential points in the existentialist view of man had
able advocates at a time when Sartre was interested in
jam from another point of view than that of existential
psychoanalysis.[5] This fact does not, of course, detract
from Sartre's ability or originality: it is a long way from
the acceptance of certain attitudes toward life to the
development of a coherent philosophical system which
justifies them, and there are important differences between existentialists. Existentialism as a movement is
much broader than any particular thinker, and would
seem to be a reflection of the spirit of the time. Such
nonphilosophers as Malraux, Bernanos, Camus, Graham
Greene, and Jean Anouilh have done perhaps more for
the diffusion of existentialist themes among the reading
and play-going public than has any technical philosopher.

Sartre's output since the War has included novels,
plays, literary criticism, biography, and essays on politics.
In spite of the controversy surrounding his work, his
reputation seems now to be firmly established as one of
the outstanding philosophers, moralists, and creative
writers of the twentieth century. The volume of his writ-

ings is already large and promises to continue to increase. Although he has not published the ethical study promised in *Being and Nothingness,* his ethics at least in outline can be determined from his later writings and from views credited to him by his associates, namely Francis Jeanson, Maurice Merleau-Ponty, and Simone de Beauvoir. Similarly, his social philosophy cannot be found in any one place, but must be gleaned from the totality of his writings. Its most explicit statement occurs in his criticism of other social doctrines, as befits an existentialist who values thinking-in-situation over abstract speculation. Sartre appears to be primarily interested in applying the insights which he derives from his philosophy to art, literature, and politics. One might add to this list himself, since he is presently engaged in writing an autobiography.

Being and Nothingness

CHAPTER II

All of Sartre's writings, his plays as well as his essays, deal with ideas. Consequently, while they may be appreciated as literature, they acquire a new dimension of meaning when related to his philosophical position. One can go from his novels to his philosophical writings to discover the explanations for character and events, or from the philosophy to the novels to find illustrations from life of his theoretical principles. Sartre expresses his personal point of view in both forms, as befits an existentialist for whom there is no separation between technical philosophy and a personal philosophy of life.

The danger, however, in relying on the literary works as sources for Sartre's ideas has resulted in much irrelevant criticism of his position. It is a mistake to take the protagonists in the novels and plays as advocates of views shared by Sartre, although this relationship between an author and his work may be fairly common. If Freud had written his study of Leonardo da Vinci in the form of a novel, it would not follow that Da Vinci's views could be ascribed to Freud. Generally speaking, Sartre's creative writing can be best understood as psychological and sociological analysis in fictional form. His ideas therefore lie behind the characters and events presented, and their interpretation depends on a knowledge of Sartre's philosophical system. Good literature is not likely to be written in the service of a philosophical system, and in criticisms of Marxist writing it is usually accepted as axiomatic that it cannot be. If Sartre is an exception to the rule, and not all agree that he is, it is probably due to the difference between Marxism and existentialism, as philosophies. The point here is not the literary quality of his works, but that Sartre would not necessarily approve of the characters which he presents or of their ideas any more than would a Marxist novelist in writing of the bourgeoisie.

Another frequently quoted supposed source for Sartre's philosophical views is the brief lecture published in the U.S. under the title *Existentialism*. In the first place, this lecture was not intended as a formulation of Sartre's philosophy as such, but rather as a description of existentialism in general. Secondly, it constitutes a popularized introduction to the subject for a lay public. An indication of the level of understanding to which Sartre was addressing himself is the reported fact that the opening reference to existentialism as a humanism provoked fainting among the audience. What can be said for the speech is that it presents some of the major conclusions of the existentialists in language which, unfortunately, can be misleading as to the actual arguments employed by Sartre in reaching such conclusions. The resulting book is therefore definitely not by itself an adequate guide to the content of his philosophy.

If one desires to discover the nature of Sartre's philosophic system, the only reliable means is to go directly to the book in which he presents its detailed development, *Being and Nothingness*. This book gives us Sartre's theory of the nature of reality, or doctrine of being. The general reader can take comfort in the fact that parts of the book are difficult even for professional philosophers, although much in it is easily accessible. In spite of the difficulty involved in the paradoxical language and unfamiliar concepts, it seems to me that the greatest barrier to the understanding of this book lies in the attitude with which many approach it. Its subject matter is supposedly universal and fundamental human experiences; its comprehension supposes a certain insight into such experiences. This insight can come only from a habit of frank and honest analysis of one's own motives and behavior. Without attempting to determine the relative rarity of such a habit or all possible reasons for its absence, certain modern traits which would militate against it seem too obvious to escape notice: a concern with activity rather than reflection, a confusion between what is and what ought to be, and a compulsive optimism about the problems of life. Those who might wish to discount these factors can perhaps explain otherwise why even psychologists and sociologists frequently fail to relate the specialized knowledge in their professional area to their personal behavior.

Jean-Paul Sartre's philosophical work, *Being and Nothingness,* bears as a subtitle "An Essay on Phenomenological Ontology." The term "phenomenological" refers to the method which is employed in this massive "essay" (651 pages, including the author's introduction in the English translation). The phenomenological method can be described as requiring an exact and careful description of phenomena as they appear to human consciousness. Such a description must dispense with all a priori principles, postulates of practical or theoretical reason, and criteria derived from authority or personal commitment. The phenomena to be described include not only sense data but also subjective emotional states, ideas, and social institutions. The act of what Sartre calls "pure reflection" can examine the emotion of fear as well as the color of chocolate. The phenomenologist seeks knowledge through a reflective analysis of that which comes within his sight and insight. All knowledge is intuitive, and the deductive method is rejected.

Sartre's system, then, is not deductive. *Being and Nothingness* is a long analysis of individual human experiences which enables conclusions to be drawn respecting the nature of consciousness and of the world, and of their relations. The result is a philosophy with a strong orientation towards psychology, and it comes as no surprise when, toward the end of his study, Sartre proposes a new form of psychoanalysis. Before writing his major philosophical work he had already established his reputation as a theorist in the field of psychology. Thus, by background and training, he was well equipped for the use of the phenomenological method.

The purpose of Sartre's investigation is to construct an ontology, or description of the being of the world and of man. He distinguishes ontology from metaphysics, which attempts to explain being in terms of its origins and purposes, by saying that metaphysics is to ontology as history is to sociology. Having restricted himself to description, which answers the question of what reality is, he can discuss the question of why reality is as he describes it by the use of the term "as if." "Ontology will therefore limit itself to declaring that *everything takes place as if* the in-itself in a project to found itself gave itself the modification of the for-itself." [1] As a description of reality, however, Sartre must claim his philosophy to be objective and of universal validity.

Because of the systematic character of Sartre's thought, a survey of the conclusions of his ontology is essential to an understanding of his criticisms of political ideologies. Although much of the worth of *Being and Nothingness* resides in the detailed analysis of particular aspects of human experience which it presents, the general outline of the ontology is fairly simple and can be briefly presented. Three splits in the unity of Sartre's universe can be discerned: that within human consciousness which includes reflective and nonreflective levels; that between consciousness and being-in-itself; that between various individual instances of consciousness which gives rise to being-for-others. These three aspects of the ontology will be discussed in order.

First, Sartre distinguishes between two kinds of mental activity, which he refers to as the Cartesian *cogito* and the prereflective *cogito*. The Cartesian *cogito* might be described as reflection on the states or actions of one's own consciousness. Consciousness turns back on itself, as it were, and questions its own activities. He goes on to conclude that reflection is simply a possibility of a nonreflective awareness which he terms the prereflective *cogito*. Consciousness is thus not a discovery of the process of reflection but rather the precondition for this process. The prereflective *cogito* is thus the primary form of consciousness for Sartre, and his analysis is aimed at elucidating its characteristics.

Through an analysis of patterns of conduct including the attitude of interrogation, the concept of destruction, and negative judgment, Sartre attempts to demonstrate that consciousness acts by negation. This is the beginning of a long argument in favor of the view that consciousness is nonsubstantial, or nothingness. Nothingness not in the sense of absence but in the sense of not being anything but a "nihilating" activity. As nothingness it is separated from the object by not being the object, and preserves a distance from it. Nevertheless, consciousness is nothing but consciousness-of-the-object and therefore presence to it. It is this that Sartre has in mind when he terms nothingness "being-for-itself"; consciousness is an awareness of being. The relation between consciousness and its object might be compared with that between a mirror and the objects which are reflected in it; the mirror has no content of its own, containing merely reflections of objects before it, yet it is always separate and never merges with the object. Descartes should have said, "I think of something" instead of simply "I think."

Human consciousness, nothingness, and being-for-itself are equivalent terms in Sartre's vocabulary. Each term represents merely a different aspect of the same phenomenon, which is called human consciousness because it is a characteristic of the individual human being, nothingness because it is a translucent awareness of something it is not, and being-for-itself because through it being becomes aware of itself. From a still different point of view it is freedom, because as nothingness it cannot be the object of determination through outside influence. Consciousness of oneself as freedom comes with the experience of anguish. "Anguish as the manifestation of freedom in the face of self means that man is always separated by a nothingness from his essence." [2]

One final aspect of the for-itself remains to be examined: that of the for-itself as desire. The for-itself is not only awareness of the object, it is also desire for it. Ultimately, the goal of the for-itself is to become substantial like the object while preserving its awareness of it. This is impossible, since that which is substantial is no longer nothing, and awareness is essentially nihilation. The view of the for-itself as desire is joined to that of the for-itself as nothingness by the concept of *lack*.

That which desires is a lack, i.e., not what it wants to be. Since the for-itself lacks everything, it is nothing.

The concept of the for-itself as desire is basic to Sartre's theory of human reality, and will be further discussed in that connection. But two important consequences of this view should be noted at this point. The first is that the fact of desire involves a project for its satisfaction. The for-itself strives toward a transcendent goal. Since the for-itself is freedom, this goal must be freely chosen. The second consequence is that the world appears valuable. That which is desired by the for-itself has value by virtue of this fact alone. Since desires are not random but organized in terms of a transcendent goal, this goal is also the source of values for the individual.

So far we have discussed the first split in Sartre's universe, that between the reflective and nonreflective levels of human consciousness, and examined the various characteristics of human consciousness, or being-for-itself. All that remains is to determine the character of the world of objects, which Sartre terms being-in-itself.

A basic distinction between being-in-itself and being-for-itself is that the former *is*, whereas being-for-itself *is not*. All consciousness is consciousness of something, of an object. Consciousness may turn back upon itself, as in the case of the Cartesian *cogito*, constituting itself as an object. In doing so it achieves a reflective awareness of its actions or states. Taken together, these psychic phenomena indicate a static unity which can be variously termed character, personality, or ego. The ego itself is thus an object of consciousness, and as such, shares the nature of the in-itself. It is, however, psychic and not material, and might better be referred to as "oneself." Consciousness may also be directed toward material objects; their existence is evident from the mere fact of their presence to consciousness, and does not require proof. The importance of Sartre's relegation of the ego to a derivative role within consciousness is evident; the ego could construct or falsify a world, but nothingness cannot. Descartes shut himself up inside the ego and required God to restore the real world to him.

The function of reflection is to examine the knowledge of the world which we have through our consciousness of it. This is what Sartre means when he says that all knowledge is intuitive. It might be said that we have direct access only to appearances. But the collection of appearances which constitutes an identifiable object *is* the object. There is no noumenal being underlying these appearances as Kant supposed.

The region of being which is composed of the objects of consciousness is termed being-in-itself because, unlike being-for-itself, it is as it appears. "Being-in-itself has no *within* which is opposed to a *without* and which is analogous to a judgement, a law, a consciousness of itself. The in-itself has nothing secret; it is solid." [3] Solid not in the sense of material, because psychic events and actions can be objects of consciousness and belong to the realm of the in-itself, but in the sense of self-identity. Apart from human consciousness the in-itself exists and has movement. Quality, such as redness, sweetness, likewise belongs to the object. But all cause, potency, particularity, purpose, and relationships with other objects, although appearing as structures of the object, are the result of the activity of the for-itself; i.e., are subjective in origin. The world as it appears to reflection is a combination of the objective characteristics of the in-itself—factual existence, solidity, quality, and movement—and

the subjective contributions of the perceiving for-itself
—particularity, order, change, value, and instrumentality.

The third split occurs through the existence of what
Sartre calls "the Other," and takes the form of a multiplicity of individual for-itselves. Insofar as the other is
merely an object in my world, he differs from other objects only in terms of his objective characteristics; i.e.,
he cannot have the status of another subject. However,
the other is also and primarily revealed to me as a subject. This revelation comes with the experience of being
an object in the world of another free, conscious being,
or what Sartre calls the experience of being a "transcendence transcended." The other appears, looks at me,
and I find myself no longer a free subjective relation to
an ideal possible state of myself. Instead I am constituted
as an ego, as a character with certain objective characteristics. While I am responsible for this "being-for-
others," in the sense that it is constructed from my behavior, I do not control it, because the meaning of this
behavior in the other's world escapes me. The being-for-
others is in fact a new dimension of my own being, my
being-as-object. New because the for-itself alone, even
by reflection, cannot grasp itself as a pure object. Nevertheless, my being for others is *my* being, and I cannot
disown it.

. . . the Other's freedom . . . is the limit of my freedom
. . . It is given to me as burden which I carry without ever
being able to turn back to know it. . . . If there is an Other
. . . then I have an outside, I have a *nature*.[4]

In short, the split between for-itselves which results in
the existence of the other person has as its consequence
a mode of being for each for-itself which is that of objective presence in the world. And in a world which is

not that of the individual for-itself, but the world of the other, which is beyond determination because of the other's freedom, and which is dangerous because beyond the control of the individual. Shame is the affective aspect of the discovery of our being-for-others. Since I either must be an object for him (masochism) or defend myself by reducing him to an object in turn (sadism), the existence of the other makes me guilty. "Thus original sin is my upsurge in a world where there are others; and whatever may be my further relations with others, these relations will be only variations on the original theme of my guilt." [5]

In summary, reality as Sartre pictures it is composed of objects and subjects, being-in-itself and being-for-itself. The category of objects includes the surrounding material world, but also any other object of consciousness, including the individual self as seen in introspection and individual behavior as seen by others, or being-for-others. The subject is consciousness, which is not essentially thinking or deliberation but rather awareness, in the sense that one can be aware or conscious of deliberating. That which exists is not subjectivity as such, but various individual instances of subjectivity. In each instance of subjectivity we find not a new kind of being but a process by which being becomes aware of itself.

Sartre's ontology embodies his attempt to find a middle way between materialism, which asserts the reality of the material world and explains the subject in terms of it, and idealism, which asserts the reality of the subject and explains the material world as the product of reason or spirit. He agrees with the materialists that objects exist apart from human experience of their existence, and he joins the idealists in holding that the nature of the world in which men live is determined by the nature of man. At the same time he avoids the dualism which makes it impossible for the subject, as one kind of being, to know the outside world, which is another. In attempting to resolve this traditional problem of philosophy, Sartre has made a contribution which has aroused much shocked criticism; namely, the identification of nothingness as the heart of human reality. This central role given to nothingness is characteristic of neither materialism nor idealism, but rather of existentialism.

This chapter has given only the briefest outline of Sartre's theory of man and the world; the concepts introduced will be examined further in later chapters in their implication for the human condition. His analysis of social and psychological phenomena depends directly on his doctrine of being or ontology, and consequently, criticisms of his position which do not attempt to answer his arguments in *Being and Nothingness* are superficial and ineffective. The systematic character of Sartre's thought has led to the accusation that Sartre is a rationalist rather than a true existentialist, since one of the main themes of existentialism has been a distrust of any attempt to encapsule individual existence within a system.

Iris Murdoch, a perceptive critic, entitles her review of the English edition of *Being and Nothingness* "Hegel in Modern Dress." [6] The accusation is that Sartre has erected a Hegelian type system, and that he has adopted some Hegelian concepts. The notion of the world as a synthesis of being (the in-itself) and nothingness (the for-itself) recalls both the structure and the conclusions of Hegelian logic. And in his discussion of being-for-others Sartre explicitly recognizes his debt to Hegel's analysis of the Master-Slave relationship in the *Phenomenology of the Mind*. Even the terms being-in-itself and being-for-itself are of Hegelian origin. A study of the influence of Hegel on Sartre would no doubt be very rewarding, but a willingness to learn from one's predecessors is hardly a disqualification for a serious philosopher. Moreover, Sartre has been accused of borrowing from many other sources besides Hegel, including Nietzsche, Kafka, Dostoevsky, Heidegger, Marx, Valéry, Ibsen, Croce, Malraux, Adler, Faulkner, Bachelard, and others.

Sartre substitutes a psychological perspective for Hegel's historical perspective, but this is not their only or their more serious divergence. The existentialist denies the basic presupposition of Hegelian idealism, namely the identification of thought and being. He adopts the descriptive rather than the deductive method. And he sides with the individual against the universal:

Here as everywhere we ought to oppose to Hegel Kierkegaard, who represents the claims of the individual as such. The individual claims his achievement as an individual, the recognition of his concrete being . . . The particular is here the support and foundation of the universal; the universal in this case could have no meaning if it did not exist for the *purpose* of the individual.[7]

Sartre's ontological categories of being and nothingness merge in the individual existent.

The concrete can be only the synthetic totality of which consciousness, like the phenomenon, constitutes only moments. The concrete is man within the world in that specific union of man with the world which Heidegger, for example, calls "being-in-the-world."[8]

And, as we shall see, Sartre's view of man within the world reflects the existentialist sense of the ambiguity of human existence and the limitations of reason which prevent any definition in advance of the meaning of history or individual existence.

The Human Condition

Sartre's social and political views are determined by his theory of the nature of the existing individual. The terms "human reality" and "human condition" are employed by Sartre in place of the more traditional term "human nature" because of what he considers to be the fundamentally ambiguous character of the existent. A presentation of Sartre's theory of human reality, despite the logical rigor of his analysis, is made difficult by this ambiguity and the added complications resulting from his unusual use of terms and taste for paradox. Consequently, even a brief discussion of his theory must distinguish his views from those that have been attributed to him by some of his critics.

It would be misleading to attempt to find in Sartre a simple definition of man, although a number of what appear to be definitions can be discovered in his work. Misleading because the fundamental condition of human reality, in the ontology as well as in the ethics, is the priority of existence over essence. Man's essence, or rationally intelligible nature, is a product of his existence and not identical with it. Existence is simple presence; beyond explanation, it sustains the essence or nature and gives it reality. Man as existent is a mystery, a paradox, and his nature and purposes cannot be summed up neatly

in any formula. It is possible to say of human reality
that, in each individual case, it *is*, but it is not possible
to say *what* it is.

Man does not live as pure existence, but he may become
aware of himself as such in the experience of *nausea*, the
subject of Sartre's first novel. The main character of the
book, Rocquentin, discovers in *nausea* that: "The essential is contingency. I mean that, by definition, existence
cannot be identified with necessity. To exist is to happen
without reason; . . . Everything is purposeless, this gar-
den, this town and myself." [1] He finds himself "astonished
before this life which is given to me—given for nothing."
Rocquentin is immobilized by the feeling that his own
life, together with all the world, is meaningless. He later
speculates on the possibility that a work of art—the creation of an artificial world of pure form—might justify his
existence.

Nausea, as experienced by Rocquentin and also
Mathieu in *The Age of Reason*, is an experience which
characterizes consciousness when it becomes aware of
itself as nothingness. Accepting this nothingness as a
fact, it no longer sees the world as ordered and valuable
but as a senseless proliferation of alien objects. This is the
experience which gives rise to the absurdity of the world
of which Sartre and Camus speak. It is possible because
of the root ambiguity of man, which is that his mental
states and past history belong to the in-itself while his
consciousness is for-itself. As for-itself an individual is
nothing, except lack of identity with the in-itself. Thus
Sartre can describe man as the being who is not what
he is and who is what he is not. Man is not what he is,
since he transcends his past by not being it in the present.
At the same time, man is what he is not in the sense of
being an undetermined future which he is not in the

present. The present is the nothingness of pure existence, and only takes on meaning in the light of the dead past or prospective future behavior. This description of human reality is at once a product of Sartre's ontology and a revelation of the individual experience of nausea.

Human reality, then, is something insofar as it is the series of individual actions which constitute a person's past history, together with those actions which are added to the past by the progressive realization of future projects. But the past and future are constantly being questioned by the nothingness of the present. Sartre's description of human reality has been found wanting by various critics. He has been accused of delighting in the absurdity of the world, and his philosophy of requiring the plight of Rocquentin. According to this view, man is left in pure nothingness and with no motives to action. However, this is not the case if we accept Sartre's comparison of his method of describing man by taking him back to the despair of nausea with the methodical doubt of Descartes. After the acceptance of absurdity, as a fact but not as a norm, Sartre moves on from the constellation of antivalues attached to contingency to a description of human life characterized by desire and value. The use of the term *nausea* to describe the experience of bare existence is a fair indication of the negative value which he assigns to it. The importance of the concept of nausea for Sartre is as a revelation of the fact that simple existence is intolerable and as such demands justification. Its unpleasant character emphasizes the need for man to give himself an essence, its possibility the fact that the essence must come from within the individual himself, as it is not given by any universal order.

Not one, but three theories of motivation have been distinguished within Sartre's theory of man. These three

theories can be termed fundamental desire, original project, and authentic existence. All three might be classified
as subjective, since they trace the source of value to the
individual consciousness. The most general theory, metaphysical in nature, is summed up in Sartre's statement
that "man fundamentally is the desire to be God." [2] What
this traditional language means within the context of the
ontology is that human consciousness by its very nature
strives toward its own appropriate end, which is a totality in which the world would be ordered by consciousness, and would thus be identical with it. But this identity
of consciousness with the world could not lead to the
destruction of either of its components; the world would
continue in its material existence, and consciousness
would retain its awareness.

It is possible to describe this spontaneous upsurge
toward a given end as a structure of human consciousness, because for Sartre the nothingness which causes the
world to appear also reveals the future. Human consciousness in its complementary roles of awareness and
desire sees the world at once as factual and as valuable—
the latter because all things appear as aids or hindrances
to the attainment of the ultimate value, which has been
termed God. But man cannot become God; Sartre compares him with the donkey who pursues a carrot which
is fixed before him on the shaft of the cart which he is
pulling.

According to this theory man must refuse absurdity.
From the moment he is aware of the world he projects an
ideal relationship to it toward which he never ceases to
strive. And all men are united in the pursuit of this same
goal. The world itself takes on meaning in the light of
man's universal and fundamental desire. Man may know
the world to be absurd apart from his projects, and he

may experience its absurdity in moments of nausea, but his life is an effort to bring order out of chaos.

While the theory of the fundamental desire to be God is seen by Sartre to be descriptive of human reality, a given historical individual is not considered to be motivated by a project of being God:

> . . . while the *meaning* of the desire is ultimately the project of being God, the desire is never *constituted* by this meaning . . . the abstract, ontological "desire to be" is unable to represent the fundamental, *human* structure of the individual; . . .[3]

We have arrived at the second theory of motivation. Sartre does not consider this theory, to which he gives the name of *original project,* an alternative to the first theory of the fundamental desire to be God. Man is nothing but what he has become through his actions, so an individual's projects must be projects not of being but of doing, making, or having. There is a considerable variety of such possible projects, and identical projects pursued within various social and historical contexts would result in diverse behaviors. On the level of human behavior, of character, and of values, the universality of man breaks down into a complex pattern of varying individual desires and social systems. These desires and systems furnish the data for an explanation of individual behavior; the "fundamental desire" is only a generalized description of what such projects have in common.

The original project is a project of realizing certain transcendent goals, which represent the ultimate values of an individual. The specific desires and motives of everyday life represent means toward the realization of the transcendent goals. This is true not only of rational or what are commonly termed conscious motivations but also of emotional impulses. An individual's ideas and emotional life are equally determined by his goal, and his essence or "nature" is determined by the project as it is continually being realized. Since particular actions represent means toward the achievement of the goal, a person grows by progressive integration. It is impossible that an individual should act in a way inconsistent with his goals, for this would imply a change in his goals. While, as we shall see, changes in goals are possible, there can be no motive for such changes, since the original project creates all causes and all motives.

The view that individual acts can be interpreted in terms of a projected ideal state of the individual is not new. The psychologist Adler had written:

. . . without worrying about the tendencies, milieu, and experiences, all psychical powers are under the control of a directive idea and all expressions of emotion, feeling, thinking, willing, acting, and dreaming, as well as psycho-pathological phenomena, are permeated by one unified life-plan.[4]

In the general perspective of Sartre's work it would seem that he also is more concerned than Adler with the relation between the individual project and the social context. Sartre refers the cataloging of the various possible original projects to future psychoanalytical investigation. He himself has written three essays in existential psychoanalysis, dealing with anti-semitism, Baudelaire, and the contemporary French writer Jean Genet. While all three are penetrating psychological studies, and explain behavior in terms of a projected vision of the self, Sartre shows a certain reticence in his first two studies when it comes to labeling projects and defining their structure.

In his study of Jean Genet, however, Sartre begins with an examination of first the circumstances and then the nature of the choice of a project, and goes on to show how Genet's subsequent behavior resulted from the pursuit of this project. Surprised in a theft at an early age, Genet chose to be the thief which he had become in the eyes of others. In other words, he chose as his goal the realization of his being-for-others, to be as a subject what he had become as an object. Sartre's analysis of Genet's development in the light of this choice is very persuasive, and it represents both an application and a further refinement of his theory of human reality. The concept of the original project as a subjective choice of goal retains the Freudian insight into prerational character of individual motivation, while avoiding the deterministic aspects of Freudian psychology. Nevertheless, the success which Sartre has had here and elsewhere in interpreting human behavior from the point of view of individual self-determination leaves open the question whether all human behavior can be so explained. Only extensive further use will show whether existential psychoanalysis is suited to the study of all human behavior or only certain aspects of it. Sartre seems to have shown that the latter use, at least, is valid.

The most controversial aspect of Sartre's theory of the original project is his contention that the project is a product of the free choice of the individual. The experience of nausea reveals not only the necessity of a project but the fact that it must be *chosen* by the individual. Every man must have an essence, but it is wholly contingent that it should be *this* essence. Because man is originally nothing, he can subsequently become anything, and whatever he has chosen to become will be final only when, after death, he no longer can change his essence. Man is "condemned to be free" because, while he did not choose to exist, once he is present in the world he is free.

There is no doubt about the importance of freedom

in Sartre's view of man, but many of his critics find that
freedom cannot be reconciled with the theory of the
original project, and accuse Sartre of being a psycho-
physiological determinist. The problem has been stated
as follows:

> Sartre appears not to recognize that if man is the "founda-
> tion without foundation" of his values and if the "foundation
> without foundation" of his values is equivalent to his funda-
> mental project of being, then this project cannot be chosen
> since it is the ultimate and irreducible fact in terms of which
> his choices are made.[5]

If man cannot choose consciously between possible al-
ternatives, his freedom is not that honored by tradition
but only a new name for necessity.

Sartre does not contend that the choice of man's fundamental project is the product of rational deliberation.

> . . . the question here is not of a deliberate choice. This is
> not because the choice is *less* conscious or *less* explicit than
> a deliberation but rather because it is the foundation of all
> deliberation and because . . . a deliberation requires an in-
> terpretation in terms of an original choice.[6]

Sartre's view that a choice can be conscious and yet not
be deliberate is merely a statement of the evaluative
aspect of that awareness of the external world which
characterizes human consciousness: "to be conscious of
ourselves and to choose ourselves are one and the same." [7]
He rejects the Freudian hypothesis of the unconscious
mind, and substitutes an evaluative awareness prior to
reflection. In support of his position he cites the comparable view of Wilhelm Steckel, Viennese psychiatrist
and pupil of Freud, who broke with Freud in finding the
roots of psychosis to be conscious. Alfred Stern finds a
coincidence between Sartre's view and the distinction
of Emil Froeschel between "not-expression-ripe" and "ex-

pression-ripe" psychic events.[8] Because of his two-level theory of consciousness, Sartre can preserve the traditional meaning of freedom, which involves the possibility of a conscious choice among possible lines of action, while accepting the Freudian emphasis on the importance of prerational motivation. Sartre can be accused of irrationalism at this point, but his assertion of man's freedom is logically compatible with the concept of the original project.

Is this kind of freedom significant for practical human purposes? What value is there in a choice of oneself from which rational deliberation is excluded? A man can change his mind on the basis of new experience, but can he change his original project? Sartre contends that he can, by means of a "radical conversion." But what is the nature of this "radical conversion"? Sartre has already said that all reasons and all motives come from the original project, and that consequently its abandonment could not be motivated. Only if this is true can an individual be regarded as an integrated personality and his past actions be understood. The meaning of this conversion phenomenon must be the key to Sartre's theory of human reality.

An explanation of the concept of conversion requires a return to the problem of the being of man as a combination of being-in-itself and being-for-itself: because of the nature of consciousness, man is not only a particular individual with given characteristics but, as nothingness, has the possibility of separating himself from these characteristics and viewing them, as it were, from a distance. This separation within an individual prevents him from merely *being* himself in any final manner and obliges him to choose himself constantly. The possibility of the experience of nausea indicates that the individual may always fall prey to the nothingness within him. In other words, consciousness must choose but cannot guarantee through time any particular choice, because it remains nothingness. The divorce from one's own project which nothingness represents is a feature of the constantly recurring present, or what Sartre terms the "instant."

Each individual decision is necessarily either a renewed choice of the same goal or a choice of new goals. Each decision requires an orientation in terms of an ultimate or goal which is continually being questioned. A decision inconsistent with the original project supposes a new transcendent goal, and gives a new meaning to the past. The drunkard who decides to go home with his pay check instead of to the bar becomes a family man and a reformed drunkard. But this new project is no more permanently guaranteed than the old, and it depends on the reaffirmation of the values presiding over this decision in future acts to confirm him as a new person.

Within the context of Sartre's theory it is impossible that the drunkard could have been determined or fated to decide as he did. Why would he so decide? Strictly speaking, this question cannot be answered, and Sartre would contend that a decision which could be explained away would not be an exercise of freedom. It is, however, possible to describe the condition which would preside over such an innovation.

The drunkard, while recognizing his old desires, must have had a vision of an open future; that is, he must have recognized his own freedom and affirmed its value. He must have been aware of the nature of his past behavior, not as simply good or bad but as *his* behavior, whose value he had long affirmed by continued practice in spite of the stresses and strains involved. Finally, he must have understood in anguish the consequences of his behavior for others, that this behavior was justified only by his own purposes and that therefore he bore the responsibility for it. Nothing could guarantee that he would act as he did, but he chose to affirm his freedom by a decision which only he could make.

The decision could of course be explained on other grounds, as for example feelings of guilt resulting from the belief that the behavior was wrong, coupled with the sickness of the wife. Which explanation would be right would depend on the actual behavior of the man in question. But if the first explanation could conceivably be correct, is it not an example of a change in goals? An original project has been modified, and the change of goals has been announced. Sartre has mentioned Raskolnikov in *Crime and Punishment* as an example of the type of conversion of which he is speaking. Paul on the road to Damascus would seem to be another such example. The cutting short by an individual of one life and the beginning of another is thus possible. The conversion which man's freedom makes possible is a change of being rather than a change of mind, an act of the whole man rather than an act of rational deliberation.

The moral significance of a conversion or its frequency is not the point to be made here. All that we need allow is its possibility. This established, Sartre's claim to defend human freedom consistently must be allowed. Man cannot act without an ideal project of himself in the world. But this project, however rationalized, is of his own choosing. This will not satisfy those who define freedom in terms of conformity to a pre-established order, but it is close enough to the traditional usage to make Sartre's use of the term legitimate.

A description of Sartre's theory of human reality in

11172899

terms of the operations of the prereflective consciousness as a self-transcending movement toward freely
chosen goals indicates the nature of man as subjectivity.
But human reality is not pure subjectivity. "The truth
is that 'human reality' 'is in society' as it 'is in the world';
it is also neither nature nor states but makes itself." [9] In
addition to an examination of man as subjectivity which
reveals how man "makes himself," something must be
said about man-in-society and man-in-the-world in order
to give an accurate picture of human reality as Sartre
sees it.

Man is in society because he finds himself to be among
other subjects, and he is in the world because he is sur-
rounded by objects. Taking the second of these two propositions first, it should be recalled that human consciousness is without content other than that derived from its
awareness of the objects which surround it, and that the
goal of consciousness is a certain relation to the world.
Thus the subject is a certain organization of the world
and can only develop by action on the world. Human
reality is "being-in-the-world" and can be defined only
in terms of its "situation." Sartre's concept of the situation is more complex than that of environment in its
usual sense. It is not the sum of the objective factors
surrounding a subject, such as economic conditions, social
standards, climate, institutions, etc., but these factors
organized and given their meaning by the goals of the
subject. The situation is a historical synthesis of the
subject and the nonsubjective conditions in which he finds
himself. Nevertheless, the subject cannot exist or be
understood in isolation from objective forces, a view
which puts Sartre in opposition to those who would give
man a substantial nature or essence which is independent

of his environment. Sartre objects to any view which represents man as self-contained, and the goal of human striving as an inner state of grace.

Man is also in society; part of our environment is made up of other people. The others, however, are more than simply objects with which we come into contact. It is true that they appear to us as object-natures, or persons having a certain character, and upon whom we pass judgments which derive from our projects. But they constitute us as objects in their turn, by virtue of their character as free subjects, and by doing so they are responsible for the creation of our "being-for-others," to which Sartre gives ontological status. This dimension of our being is revealed to us by the look of the other, and we are responsible for the nature which the other gives by his look in the sense that our behavior is the source of the other's judgment of us. Shame is the emotion which reveals to us both the presence of the other and the fact that what is seen is ourselves. "Shame is by nature *recognition.* I recognize that I *am* as the Other sees me." [10] Human reality includes not only our subjectivity but also ourselves as objective existents, and it is through the other person that we are faced with the necessity of passing judgment on ourselves.

. . . each of my free conducts engages me in a new environment where the very stuff of my being is the unpredictable freedom of another [which constitutes my being-for-others]. Yet by my very shame I claim as mine that freedom of another. I affirm a profound unity of consciousnesses, . . . for I accept and wish that others should confer upon me a being which I recognize.[11]

Similarly, a group is constituted as such by the presence of a third who sees its members as objects. The recognition of the being or nature which the presence of another subject reveals to us is felt as shameful because its being as an object is judged from the point of view of the other's goals and not our own.

Thus the individual is for Sartre social, not in the sense that he fits harmoniously into the collectivity, but in the sense that his reality as an individual is mediated through the other members of the collectivity.

It is not in I don't know what retreat that we will discover ourselves: it is on the road, in the city, among the crowd, thing among things, man among men.[12]

Social life is accompanied by considerable stress and strain since the individual is inevitably degraded by being considered as a mere object. Sartre's analysis of relations with others in *Being and Nothingness* is an account of the conflicts which result when individuals attempt to escape from this difficult situation by various evasive tactics, all of which are finally futile. The social nature of man appears unpleasant and at the same time inevitable, and interpersonal conflict as a necessary ingredient of all social relationships.

. . . as for absolute reciprocity, it is masked by historical conditions of class and race, by nationalities, by the social hierarchy; a chief is never an object for his subordinates or else he is lost; he is rarely a subject for his superiors. So we live, ordinarily, in a sort of familiar and unconscious indistinction: one passes unnoticed; in the profession, in the family, in the party, we are neither altogether objects or subjects. The Other is the instrument who obeys our voice, who shares, distributes and is, at the same time, this warm and diffuse presence which surrounds us; . . .[13]

In this quotation the harshness of the interpersonal struggle characteristic of Sartre's philosophical study is softened by the privileges, duties, established routines and occasional privacy of social life. Human reality includes the possibility of solitude, where subjectivity can have relatively free play, and life in society, where the objective nature is dominant. The life of the individual is a tension between these two poles, neither of which offers a permanent refuge.

In describing Sartre's theory of human reality, we have said that man is his project, which is the key to all his behavior; that he is free, and can change his life; that he is a product of his own actions and situation; and, finally, that he is as others see him. These are not simply aspects of human life or things which can be said about particular individuals, but categories in a definition of human reality. They do not, however, define human nature, or all of the traits which go to make up a particular individual personality. On the level of human nature there is not man, there are men. And each man is what he makes of himself. This description of human reality indicates the materials which men everywhere have to work with in the process of self-construction. We have to do not with human nature but with the human condition.

It is easy to see at this point why Sartre speaks of the ambiguous character of human reality, and why he distrusts the notion of personality. Where, among all these disparate elements, are we to look for the personality of a particular individual? Many writers have thought that Sartre's devaluation of personality, or what is even worse of "character," was a conclusive argument against the soundness of his doctrine. They are supported by the viewpoint of ordinary language, which conditions us to think of ourselves as "I," a word which carries implications of self-identity, as if we were to think of ourselves as apples or pears. The question is whether "I" is a reality, or simply a shorthand term for a much more complicated structure.

In fact, Western man has long been used to thinking of himself as composed of at least two elements, mind and body, a dualism which was extended to the personality itself in terms of the reason–passion dichotomy. Modern man, after Freud, has become more or less accustomed to thinking of himself as a trinity: id–ego–superego. The concept of personality in the Freudian framework can at best refer to an unstable equilibrium of these frequently conflicting entities. Thus limited, the concept of personality could also find a place within Sartre's system, in spite of the differences between his theory and that of Freud. However, Sartre himself prefers more dynamic terms than "personality," undoubtedly due to its tendency to hide the multidimensionality, freedom, and goal-seeking which his theory ascribes to human reality. All existentialists would be inclined by their views to be suspicious of the term as lending a spurious unity and identity to the individual. The ambiguity of Sartrean man would not seem to be an important argument against this version of the human condition.

The constituent elements of human reality in Sartre's theory are the for-itself, which is at once freedom and a project toward the attainment of goals, and the in-itself, which includes the material and social conditions which form an individual's "situation" and his past actions. The latter can be considered either from the point of view of the other, in which case they constitute his being-for-others, or from the individual's own point of view, as constituting his self. Sartre's preference for terms of philosophical origin over more commonly accepted terms in his description of human reality tends to obscure the fact that his concepts have much similarity to some of those currently employed by social scientists. A brief discussion of Sartre's points of agreement with contemporary psychologists and sociologists should both clarify the meaning of some of these concepts and indicate that they are supported by considerable factual evidence.

Among the basic concepts of psychoanalysis are those of psychic determinism, the unconscious, and the significance of early childhood in personality development. First discovered by Freud, these principles are now generally accepted by psychoanalysts and social scientists. Sartre's ideas definitely belong to the post-Freudian tradition, in spite of important differences between the two. In the first place, Sartre explicitly disagrees with Freud's concept of the unconscious in his discussion of the for-itself: he maintains that the unconscious is in fact conscious. However, he reintroduces a two-level split within consciousness, the prereflexive *cogito* and the level of rational deliberation. This resembles the Freudian concept of the unconscious in that it postulates a layer of personality which is not readily available to reflection and allows for motives unknown to the ego. For both Freud and Sartre the prerational level is the seat of desire, and repression a possible defense against desire. By insisting that repression is an activity of consciousness, Sartre presents the self-deception involved in denying that one has a desire which is actually present, as in the case of repression, as a voluntary act rather than as an occurrence over which one has no conscious control.

According to the concept of psychic determinism, individual behavior is not a series of random responses to different external stimuli, but a whole of which each specific action reveals an aspect of a basic internal structure. The individual is conceived of as a totality, and all his behavior as expressive of a basic attitude toward life. Sartre expressly adopts this Freudian view, with the difference that he, in company with Adler, explains actions as determined by projected goals rather than by habitual reactions originating in childhood experiences. However, in his study of Jean Genet, Sartre traces the adoption of the project to such an experience; Sartre's project begins at a point of time in childhood when the individual becomes for the first time aware of himself as a separate entity and projects a desired relationship between himself and the world. He has not been too definite on this point, but it would seem that the emergence of the project would coincide with the progressive formation, in terms of Freudian psychology, of the superego. For the Freudian the id is present from birth, while first the ego and then the superego are gradually developed through experience. Both Sartre and Freud apparently agree that for a period of time in infancy individuality is not yet present, and there is during this period a lack of conscious separation of the child from his environment. Likewise, they agree that the behavior of an adult stems from a basic and largely irrational attitude toward his environment.

The view that individual behavior is organized around the pursuit of obligatory goals is also found in the field of sociology; the concept of anomy, originating with Durkheim, indicates a condition where such goals are not present—resulting in disorganization of individual personalities and social decline. Durkheim does suppose that these goals are of social origin, that they furnish a basis for social unity and are inculcated into individuals at an early age. Sartre would assert that goals vary and are privately adopted; still, individual goals in his system are formulated in terms of a particular social environment, and while they involve the modification of that environment they also suppose it.

Finally, another sociological concept that finds a parallel in Sartre's theory is that of status, with the associated concept of role playing. These concepts, originating with, among others, George Herbert Mead, are considered by sociologists to be revelatory of a major aspect of social reality and determinant of individual behavior. The status of an individual is determined by the manner in which he is regarded by others; status is associated with profession but cannot be reduced to it. The status of a particular individual will vary from group to group, and supposedly even from person to person, although one can speak loosely of an individual's "social status." The individual finds that in order to act in society he is obliged to assume the roles which others set for him by their expectations, or in other words, by his status. It is not difficult to recognize here Sartre's concept of being-for-others, the dimension of human reality which, although alien to the individual, must be assumed by him.

This brief discussion of certain connections between Sartrean theory and contemporary empirical science does not exhaust the subject. Much more could be said about such matters as Sartre's rejection of Freud's topological division of the human personality into id, ego, and super-ego, for example. This aspect of Freud's theory, as well as other aspects, is a subject of current controversy between psychoanalysts, and Sartre's view here represents one possible approach to the matter. The problem of the role within Sartre's theory of other concepts widely employed by the social sciences could well be raised, but since Sartre has not addressed himself to this problem, it is perhaps not wise to do so. It seems to me, however, that Sartre's theory of human reality has very much in common with the view of man inherent in the empirical sciences, although the complexity of this question is indicated by the fact that none of the specialized sciences claim to present a total explanation of human being. This description of Sartre's position may be surprising to those who look on existentialism as a strictly philosophical enterprise or a reformulation of traditional religious views; but it is in my opinion important for the understanding of Sartre's orientation and the content of his doctrine to view his position in relation to the contributions of contemporary social science with respect to the human condition.

Freedom as an Ethics

CHAPTER IV

The passage from an ontological description of human reality to an ethical theory can be risky. It requires the transition from a more or less static analysis of the being of man to an explanation of his relation to transcendent goals. If man is presented as naturally depraved, it becomes difficult to show why he would be inclined to act morally. If he is presented as naturally good, then it would seem inevitable that he should so act. The most conflicting views have been expressed on the subject of Sartre's ethics; at one extreme it is asserted that the primary concern of existentialists since Kierkegaard is ethical and at the other it is contended that Sartre's ontology is a formulation of nihilism. In between these two extremes fall those who claim that Sartre has an ethics, but that it is merely an afterthought designed to placate his critics and bears no essential connection to his philosophy. Those who hold this view generally refer to his published speech on existentialism for his ethical views and find them inconsistent with the picture of man presented in *Being and Nothingness*.

The position taken here is that Sartre has an ethics, and that it is consistent with the rest of his philosophy. His ethical views represent a development of his thought which is subsequent to the ontology, although they have never been systematically developed in any of Sartre's published works. Yet enough evidence is available to discern at least the outline of his position, both in his own works and in the writings of Simone de Beauvoir and Francis Jeanson, who because of their relationships with Sartre can be regarded as privileged interpreters. And Sartre's ethics does not seem to be a mere afterthought: the step from his ontology to his ethics seems to be more than simple deduction from a philosophical position accepted in advance. For example, his use of an analysis of "bad faith" to reveal the nature of being-for-itself would seem likely, as the term itself suggests, to have followed upon a prior interest in "bad faith" as a moral phenomenon. This possibility seems to be borne out by the important place which "bad faith" holds in his ethical doctrine. Sartre's description of the being of man can be considered to contain an implicit moral critique of human attitudes and behavior. Indeed, he has been accused of charging with moral significance aspects of human behavior and mental life which more traditional psychologists have long struggled to render morally neutral. It is a mistake to take Rocquentin of *Nausea,* Mathieu of *The Age of Reason,* and to some extent even Orestes of *The Flies* as examples of Sartre's ethical ideal. Nevertheless, probably the best source for Sartre's ethical views are his dramatic works, which contain the quasi-totality of his themes. The personage of Hoederer in *Dirty Hands* probably comes closest to being a representation of Sartre's ethical ideal.

The most evident of the ethical conclusions to be drawn from Sartre's description of human reality, which can, for present purposes, be summed up by the statement that man is a free being, deals with what ethics cannot be. The fact of human freedom means that ". . . in the bright realm of values, we have no excuse behind us, nor justification before us." [1] No excuse behind us, because only our own free choice can account for our actions. Under the heading of "excuses" can be put all theories which interpret man's behavior in terms of some natural or supernatural deterministic system—fate, the will of God, the promptings of the unconscious or the prodding of external stimuli. The popular beliefs that we can be determined to a particular course of action by either the pattern of our past conduct—our "personality"—or by the influence of our environment—the admonitions of our parents—are equally fallacious.

Similarly, our freedom rules out the possibility of a justification before us. Values are valid only because we have chosen them as valuable. We can change our values by our own decision, and there are no omens in the world to which we can turn to know that we have decided rightly. The belief that the approval of another or of society in general can justify our actions is fallacious, as is the belief that universally valid moral absolutes exist. Nor is there a transcendent self to which we can look for directives; our transcendence is a function of our present choices which are freely made.

Holding fast to the illusions of excuse and justification is characteristic of those individuals who seek to hide their freedom from themselves. *Les lâches* hide themselves behind norms and reasonings which serve them as excuses, while *les salauds* appeal to objective moral standards or necessity to justify their aggressive self-assertion. Both of these types are examples of what Sartre terms, using the word serious in a pejorative sense, the "serious" mentality. They seek to hide from themselves the fundamental ambiguity of human reality, which is a paradoxical combination of being-in-itself and being-for-itself.

The serious man seeks to smother the nothingness of being-for-itself by immersion in being-in-itself. This does not necessarily require a denial of transcendent goals; only that the goals of the project be regarded as necessary and not as a free choice of the individual. This is equivalent to regarding being-for-itself as a thing, or being-in-itself. Sartre also recognizes a secondary form of seriousness, in which the individual, fearful of compromising himself by an act which would launch him into the realm of being-in-itself, takes refuge in the nothingness of being-for-itself. Such is the case of Mathieu in *The Age of Reason* who cannot decide to commit himself in marriage or politics.

Persons who, in whatever way, refuse to accept freedom on the level of practical reason and to live according to the reality of the human condition are guilty, according to the usual terminology of existentialism, of unauthenticity. Sartre prefers to speak of lack of commitment; he also uses the terms "bad faith" and "sincerity." A person is in "bad faith" if he declines to accept the fact that he is what he is, namely his past actions, present decisions, and projected future. A person is "sincere" if he refuses to admit that he is not what he is, denying his freedom and regarding himself as a personality with a given role in society. Sartre's analyses of unauthentic types are of a remarkable virtuosity, and represent one of the chief values of his work.

To say that man lacks excuse or justification is just another way of saying that man makes himself, and therefore, is responsible for what he is. ". . . existentialism's first move is to make every man aware of what he is and to make the full responsibility of his existence rest on him." [2] We are not responsible for being in the world, but we cannot avoid responsibility for the role which we have chosen to play in the world. The chief characteristics of Sartre's ethical position so far described can be summed up briefly in the following points: the individual, in an isolation imposed upon him by his freedom and in response to the requirements of his unique situation, must make his moral choices and bear responsibility for them; there are no acts which are good or bad in themselves, no goals that are automatically worthy; there are no structures of physical nature, reason, or history above which man cannot rise freely by his self-transcending consciousness of himself. Thus far Sartre's ethics does not differ materially from that of more traditional thinkers, Reinhold Niebuhr for example.

What is new in Sartre's ethics is his version of the existentialist virtue of authenticity, which replaces the Christian love commandment. Authenticity requires of man not a code of conduct but a way of life. An ethics based on an essentialist view of man tends to take the form of universally valid content-filled norms, or specific rules of conduct, which Sartre cannot and does not admit. Instead he emphasizes the obligation to live in a certain way. The term existence as used by Sartre therefore sometimes takes on a second meaning, that of true or authentic existence as opposed to the absurd existence revealed by the experience of nausea: ". . . man is constantly outside of himself; in projecting himself, in losing himself outside of himself, he makes for man's existing; and, on the other hand, it is by pursuing transcendent goals that he is able to exist; . . ." [3] Existence here is equivalent to the pursuit of transcendent goals, an important part of the authentic life.

Authentic existence is directly related to the being of man. It is a way of life which is in accordance with a

realistic grasp of the ambiguous nature of human reality.
". . . authenticity is a kind of honesty or a kind of courage; the authentic individual faces something which the
unauthentic individual is afraid to face." [4] That which he
faces is the ambiguous character of human reality; the
fact that he is nothing apart from his actions, the necessity to pursue transcendent goals, the realization that
these goals are of his own choice and that he is responsible for what he has done in their pursuit. In short, he
must face his freedom and the anguish which accompanies this revelation.

Whatever may be the case for other existentialists,
Sartre does not appear to envisage authenticity as simply
the acceptance of a certain attitude toward human reality
and the world. This is of course necessary, and he says
that man must assume his freedom. But true existence is
something beyond the assumption of an attitude; it is
the making of free decisions.

. . . if man has once become aware that in his forlornness he
imposes values, he can no longer want but one thing, and
that is freedom, as the basis of all values. That doesn't mean
that he wants it in the abstract. It means simply that the ultimate meaning of the acts of honest men is the quest for
freedom as such.[5]

There is no doubt that Sartre finds it impossible to make
a distinction between freedom and free acts. The free
man is not distinguished by his beliefs, but by the quality
of his actions. Thus Sartre speaks rarely of authenticity
and constantly of engagement, by which he means free
commitment to a course of action.

Commitment has two aspects, subjective and objective.
The subjective aspect of commitment is substantially the
requirement that one act authentically. It requires that

one accept responsibility for his past within the context of a project of surpassing it toward a given future. In nonphilosophic terms:

Once a man has become self-conscious . . . he is morally obliged to act in no way that will deaden his preoccupation with his integrity. He is obliged to impregnate all his actions with some sense of their relevance to him, as a man and as a person.[6]

The objective aspect of commitment is derived from the fact that an act is essentially a relation between the actor and the world. Problems of action therefore include problems of the nature of society and history, the relation of means to ends, and the consequences of action.

A man cannot become the person he wants to be merely by thinking about himself, but only by doing something with himself. This requires involving himself in the affairs of others, in adapting himself to social pressures, in transforming his environment, . . .[7]

Thus Hoederer in *Dirty Hands* is willing to lie because he is interested in changing a society which is built upon lies. Because of the conditions under which action must take place commitment means not a sudden spectacular gesture but long-term commitment to a cause. Such commitment, however, can never be final, and is constantly accompanied by anguish. If Sartre condemns seriousness, he is also unhappy with moral acrobats, who must prove their virtue by a constant pursuit of temptation. In *Kean* the idol of London society leaves for a peaceful but no less authentic domestic life in the exile of America. Hoederer illustrates how authenticity is compatible with the discipline of a revolutionary party.

What has been termed the objective aspect of commitment, besides being important in defining the nature

of personal commitment, is one of the paths which lead
to Sartre's social ethics. Man is not only in-the-world but
in-society. Sartre contends that since we are necessarily
involved with others, we are responsible for all men,
not just for our own individuality. The recognition of
freedom and its concomitant responsibility is accompanied by anguish. The anguish of the military leader,
who orders an attack in which men will be killed, is a
permanent condition of all human action. Whether it is
anguish at the thought of the consequences for ourselves
or at the recognition that our acts have consequences for
others makes little difference. There are no purely self-
regarding acts.

One writer has contended that Sartre's view in *Existentialism* that one chooses for all is not characteristic of
his work as a whole and is not adequately presented in
the one place where he does mention it. Since it is this
view which has been credited to Sartre in the preceding
paragraph, it should be pointed out that Sartre does in
fact develop it in more detail elsewhere, and that it is
an outgrowth of his theory of human reality. Sartre dis-
cusses the subject of responsibility in *Being and Nothingness,* and states that ". . . the responsibility of the
for-itself extends to the entire world as a peopled-world.
It is precisely thus that the for-itself apprehends itself
in anguish; . . ." [8] Sartre's position has been described
as follows:

. . . Sartre gives a quite special meaning to his dictum that,
in authentic choice, the individual is also choosing for other
people. It is not merely a reformulation of the ethical com-
monplace that man is a political animal. Its primary basis is
ontological. If the fundamental project of the self is to constitute its world, then it cannot choose for itself without determining the relative positions of other selves within its own
world. Having care for other men is the same as having care

for . . . one's perspective, insofar as it involves other selves as constituent factors. They must be ordered as objects gathered about the primary subject or free self.[9]

This analysis is not inconsistent with the view that relations with others are characterized by conflict, since the other is a subject in his turn, has his own world, and can look at us as objects. In other words, the being-for-others which our look identifies as the other-object will not be the same as his subjective apprehension of himself, nor will our world be his. This ambiguity cannot be avoided. Nevertheless, our apprehension of the place we have given another in our world is accompanied by anguish, as it is a function of our own unjustifiable aims or purposes.

This notion of responsibility cannot by itself serve as the basis for a social ethics; it confines itself to establishing the ". . . existence around us of a charged field, and where all our acts acquire immediately the character of merits and of demerits. To live is to awake in bonds, as Gulliver in Lilliput . . ."[10] It raises the problem of the adequacy of our acts to our intentions, but because others are considered as objects they remain means and not ends. At the same time the fact that the other is free subjectivity and can reduce us to objects in his turn means that our version of the common good is contested by that of the other. There is no standard of the social welfare which flows automatically from all individual subjectivities. The for-itself cannot be social in "nature," as it has no nature. Instead, it must create its relation to society in the same way that it creates its own individuality.

Sartre's social ethics only begins with this notion of responsibility for others. The key to his social ethics is what he refers to in *Existentialism* as the world of "inter-

subjectivity." The concept of inter-subjectivity originates
in Sartre's discussion of being-for-others in *Being and
Nothingness*. My existence as an object, or as being-for-
others, is only possible in the presence of other subjects.
At the same time my own subjectivity has as an aspect
of its project what might be termed my being-among-
others, that is, my intentions for my social being. Ideally,
my being-among-others and being-for-others should coincide, so that I am objectively what I intend to be sub-
jectively. This is never wholly possible, however, because
the goals of my subjectivity and the goals of the subjectivity of the other diverge, and my behavior is regarded from two different points of view. Thus Sartre
can say:

. . . the man who becomes aware of himself through the
cogito also perceives all others, and he perceives them as the
condition of his own existence. He realizes that he can not
be anything (in the sense that we say that someone is witty
or nasty or jealous) unless others recognize it as such. . . .
The other is indispensable to my own existence, as well as
to my knowledge about myself.[11]

Even the attempt to reduce another person to the status
of an object, thereby asserting the dominance of one's
own subjectivity, is dependent upon an acceptance of
one's own being-for-others. The torturer asserts his superiority over his victim, who is reduced to an object
subservient to his will. But he can do so only by accepting his role as torturer. If he refuses to identify himself
with the role assigned by his status, he would lose all
contact with and control over the other. In the case of
torture, however, Sartre considers such an identification
to be impossible. The victim's judgment of the torturer
is not something which the latter can in fact accept, and
sadism is possible only because of the possibility of bad

faith. What this example illustrates is the domain of inter-subjectivity, where every subject is dependent on others for the realization of his project for himself.

Our intentions and the judgments which others make of us never coincide:

We all hide, deep within ourselves, a scandalous rupture . . . we know all the anguish of being wrong and not being able to consider ourselves in the wrong, of being right and not feeling ourselves right; we all oscillate between the temptation to prefer ourselves to all because our consciousness is for us the center of the world and that of preferring everything to our consciousness; . . .[12]

Sartre would have us yield to neither temptation, but to direct our actions so as to bring our social being into line with our intentions. This is feasible because we know enough of others to look at ourselves from their point of view. The ultimate in this direction would be to subject them to existential psychoanalysis, but this is unnecessary for practical purposes because the immediate demands of their projects can be ascertained in terms of the situation which we share with them; the minimum demand of the unemployed is work, and of the Jew to live his life free of persecution.

The basis of Sartre's idea of social obligation can thus be found in the look of the other members of society, and particularly of those members whose judgment of us is the most harsh—the underprivileged. Society at any given time appears to the authentic individual, in response to the look of the underprivileged, as oppression calling out to be remedied. The particular remedies of which the common good is composed depend on the historical circumstances. It is in this context that we can understand Sartre's assertion that "I can take freedom as my goal only if I take that of others as a goal as well." [13] The free act of Orestes in *The Flies* depends for its meaning on the people of Argos.

In the pursuit of the social welfare as a means to individual welfare there is a reciprocity of subject to subject, united by the goal which is sought in common, which does not appear in Sartre's discussion of interpersonal relationships in *Being and Nothingness*. This does not result from inconsistency, but rather from development of his thought. *Being and Nothingness* is a description and denunciation of a world of conflict where hell is other people. This world was France under the Occupation, where social action was impossible, the Resistance, as Sartre says, being only an individual solution. *Existentialism* announced without explaining a shift in emphasis from solitary suffering to concrete enterprises of reform.

In addition to the argument that man can make himself only under the gaze of another, Sartre contends that authenticity requires that we should do unto others as we would have them do unto us. He argues in effect that while there are no universal and objective norms, once we adopt a norm for ourselves we must will it to be of universal validity. For example, if a man wishes to be told the truth he cannot lie himself; by the act of lying he would affirm the desirability of a world of liars. Although Sartre's discussion of this subject is brief, his view appears to be that the authentic man will know that norms are not merely general principles governing desirable personal behavior, but commitments to a given state of the world. One who postulates a world without liars as a moral ideal cannot consistently lie himself. This formalistic argument fits strangely into Sartre's voluntarism; it may be that a rational grasp of the nature of human reality would lead man to live his condition rather than flee it, but it is hard to see how considerations of rational consistency could create moral obligation. Perhaps the brief passage in *Existentialism* should be taken in a descriptive rather than a normative sense. While Sartre denies that there are universal values *prior* to the free choice of the existing individual, he does regard the production of values as the essential task of the individual consciousness. Freedom separates the individual from constituted values by negation, but it also has the positive task of creating new values by which to measure the old.

Thus, by taking part in our unique period, we finally rejoin the eternal, and our task as a writer is to illuminate the eternal values which are implied in its social and political debates. But we will not try to look for them in a sheltering sky: they are only significant in their present form. Far from being relativists, we affirm strongly that man is an absolute. But he is such at his hour, among his associates, in his homeland.[14]

The existing individual is for Sartre a set of relations between his past, present, and future, other people and the world. Sartre likes to quote Heidegger's description of man as a being of distances, a restless energy whose poles are the futurity of his project, the freedom of the instant, the world and other persons. All these vectors intersect at a point which is the free act of the individual. Sartre's social ethics resembles his personal ethics in that the obligation is to a way of living, this time of social life. The individual must assume responsibility for his society and has a duty to work for its improvement. No social state is a priori worthy; all societies are in need of improvement, and a social state of static perfection is illusory.

Sartre's ethics may be summarized as the obligatory

pursuit of chosen ends, accompanied by a constant awareness that they are freely chosen and that a new choice is
possible. It requires both action and uncertainty, activity
and reflection, modes of life which have often been held
to be incompatible. Authenticity seems to involve a personal development remarkably similar to that envisioned
by Freud; the prerational desires of the individual are
brought within the area of intelligent action, and adapted
to the rationally determined demands of the individual
in relation to his environment. Another significant comparison, in addition to that with Freud, can be made
between the Sartrean ethics and that of the stoics. While
the stoics called upon the individual to learn to accept
a frequently unpleasant external world, Sartre calls upon
him to learn to live with the desire, shame, and anguish
inherent in the human condition. The result is an ethics
which maintains a healthy skepticism toward what
Niebuhr refers to as ". . . the Phariseeism which im-
agines that we can lift ourselves above the tragic moral
ambiguities of our existence by a simple act of the will." [15]
A movement of the will subsequent to rational deliberation may be the servant of unauthenticity. Only if we
have once understood the nature of our freedom and felt
in anguish our responsibility can rational decision attain
the stature of personal commitment. And even then ethics
must be primarily concerned with the relation of means
to ends, of acts to their consequences, the final goals
constantly in question and perpetually beyond reach.

Before leaving the subject of Sartre's ethics, it should
be noted that he has frequently been accused of inconsistency for insisting that the individual has an obligation to assume his freedom, or, put another way, that
once man has become conscious of his freedom he must
recognize it as valuable. According to Alfred Stern:

. . . the absolute value which he ascribes to authenticity and sincerity cannot be justified by his own philosophy; for we know that the latter does not admit any value of supra-individual validity, given before an individual choice. . . . According to this philosophy, the acceptance of the absolute value of authenticity could even be characterized as a manifestation of unauthenticity, that is of the spirit of seriousness, which considers values as transcendent data . . . so it would seem that only through a fortunate inconsequence of his philosophy does the latter escape nihilism and become an irrationalistic absolute idealism.[16]

Irrationalistic because as a value freedom brings with it not peace but anguish. It has been noted that authenticity is life lived according to the nature of human reality, and that life can also be an attempt to evade the requirements of the human condition. How can Sartre found the value of authenticity?

Sartre cannot, as Stern points out, hold that authenticity is an absolute value of universal validity. But it is not at all clear that he does. Since Sartre denies the validity of so-called a priori moral principles it must be assumed that he does not intend to assert one, if his philosophy can justify it on an alternate basis. The answer appears to be that for Sartre the assumption of the human condition is rational, and that an individual is most likely to move in the direction of the integration of his personality and the progressive realization of his goals if his efforts are based on a rational understanding of the human condition. In *The Devil and the Good Lord* Goetz, who unintentionally has brought on a war by his futile effort to do good through selflessness, assumes the war as his responsibility and enters authentic existence at the head of a peasant army. Whatever the risks of authenticity, Sartre apparently feels that they are less to be feared than self-defeating evasion of the human condition. Since this condition is universal, and all men can experience the anguish which reveals it, the assumption of freedom is open to all.

Stern's view that authenticity is irrational because anguish accompanies it is based on the assumption that rationality commands a static happiness. Such happiness is impossible for the authentic or unauthentic within the context of Sartre's philosophy. If anguish recalls the authentic man to his freedom and responsibility, the despair of nausea awaits the unauthentic. Also, since rationality is necessary to the effective pursuit of any way of life, the attempt to compartmentalize reason will lead either to inefficient action or the revelation of inconvenient facts. Sartre appears to believe that the admission of the absurdity of the world and the fact that man makes himself will make the human condition easier to bear.

The Impossible God

CHAPTER V

A consideration of Sartre's criticism of Catholic ideology encounters immediately the much publicized fact of his declared atheism.

We are accustomed to taking disbelief in God rather for granted among social thinkers. As early as the eighteenth century atheism was widespread and at times fashionable. The tradition of atheism has since been maintained by such men as Karl Marx, Auguste Comte, and John Dewey, to name only a few of those most influential upon social thought. For most social theorists atheism meant a rejection of the idea of God as an unnecessary hypothesis for men engaged in an attempt to understand social phenomena through the methods of science and by the light of reason.

In the case of Sartre, however, there are some complicating factors. Existentialism as a philosophy has a strong religious orientation: Søren Kierkegaard, the "founder" of existentialism, was a religious reformer, and such prominent existentialists as Berdyaev, Karl Jaspers, and Gabriel Marcel are also religious thinkers. Even Heidegger, whose name has been linked with that of Sartre as the other prominent representative of the atheistic branch of existentialism, has been claimed for the ranks of the faithful. Sartre himself has denied that

there is any necessary connection between existentialism
and atheism:

> . . . Existentialism formerly, with Kierkegaard, went hand in
> hand with religious faith. French existentialism today tends
> to be accompanied by a declaration of atheism, but that is
> not absolutely necessary . . .[1]

An understanding of Sartre's atheism is further complicated by the fact that he frequently employs religious
terminology, in his philosophical as well as in his literary
works. For example, he states that ". . . man fundamentally is the desire to be God."

At the same time, he does not hesitate to assert his
atheism when engaged in polemics or popular discussion
of his doctrine. Gabriel Marcel reports with disapproval
that Sartre, descending from his plane on a visit to Swit-
zerland, greeted the waiting reporters with the statement
that "God is dead." Sartre sees his atheism as heavy with
consequences. He describes his doctrine as "an attempt
to draw all the consequences of a coherent atheistic position." It would thus seem suitable to present Sartre's
views on Catholicism in terms of his atheistic position
and the consequences which ensue from his denial of
God.

Sartre takes as his idea of God the definition offered by
Catholic theology. God is, according to the definition, the
being who is what he wants to be, or in the usual Latin
phrase *ens causa sui*. Sartre, translating this expression
into the categories of his ontology, defines God as being-
in-itself-for-itself, or the self-conscious totality of being
which founds its being through consciousness of itself.
For the Catholic this definition of God is the answer to
the question of why the world exists, and embodies the
assumption that philosophic reason is capable of answer-

ing this question. The Catholic argument for the existence of God falls into that branch of philosophy which
is traditionally called metaphysics and explains being
in terms of its causes.

The primary purpose of *Being and Nothingness* is the
description of being, a project which Sartre assumes to
be within the realm of human experience. He refers to
this description as an ontology, and distinguishes it from
metaphysics which would explain what he restricts himself to describing. He asserts that metaphysics deals with
a realm beyond human experience, and that therefore
certainty is impossible in this area. Technically, therefore, it would seem that Sartre should be classified as an
agnostic. He does, however, develop some hypotheses
about metaphysical questions, prefacing his views with
the qualification "as if." It is in the course of these specu-
lations that he comes to the conclusion that the existence
of God is "impossible," which should be read as unlikely
since he rules out certain knowledge in this domain.
What he essentially does is to say that if reason was
competent to undertake the exposition of first causes,
God would not exist.

Scattered through *Being and Nothingness* can be found
arguments of this nature. They are all conditioned by
the descriptions which Sartre has given of being-in-itself
and being-for-itself. Being-in-itself possesses reality, and
is what it appears to be. Being-for-itself, or "nothingness," is synonymous with present human consciousness.
Sartre describes consciousness as acting by negation, by
which he means that it can take notice of an object only
by being at the same time aware that it is not the object.
For example, the identification of this book as a book
requires a questioning attitude, an awareness that this
book might not be a book at all. Nothingness is that part

of human reality which liberates man from the world of objects and is thus the source of his freedom. Sartre's emphasis is on the fact that being-for-itself is able to reveal being-in-itself because it is nothingness, or lack of being. Now, we have pointed out that the idea of God is that of a being whose consciousness of himself would be identical with his nature as existent; he would coincide with himself. The difficulty of conceiving a union of being with lack of being is evident, and Sartre insists that such a union is impossible. If consciousness became identified with being-in-itself, and thus ceased to stand at a distance from it, consciousness would lose its distinctive character, and thus go out of existence. Sartre presents several detailed arguments to prove that the idea of God is self-contradictory and therefore impossible, but we shall consider only the three dealing with the possibility of an idea of God consistent with human freedom.

Sartre argues that if man in his inner being is not dependent on God, then he has no "need" for a Creator. "If Creation is an original act and if I am shut up against God, then nothing any longer guarantees my existence to God; he is now united to me only by a relation of exteriority, as the sculptor is related to the finished statue, . . ." [2] Of course, if man was dependent upon God in a continuing sense, he would not be an independent existent, and could not be free. Second, it is no solution to say that God has given man an essence, and that he is free to act in accordance with it. Freedom requires that man's acts be self-determined, and that he choose his own essence. Finally, Sartre considers the argument that God could be considered to choose our essence, while leaving us free, by determining the time of our death and thus depriving us of the opportunity for

further acts which might change our essence. Garcin in
No Exit dies as a coward, and thus becomes a coward in
a final sense which would not have been possible if he
had lived. There would have been the possibility of his
changing his essence by an act of courage. Sartre agrees
that our death is the end of our freedom, and the point
at which the individual becomes in a complete and final
sense what he has been. But God cannot have this power
without human freedom becoming meaningless. For it is
the future which gives meaning to the present, and if
the future is cut off, the present cannot admit free action.
If Verlaine had died before writing his poems, he would
not have been a great poet but a vagrant; the power to
determine the time of death would be equivalent to the
power to determine the meaning of life itself.

These arguments are undoubtedly important for Sartre
because of the primary value that he places on freedom, and the central role that it occupies in his ontology.
The problem of reconciling free will and determinism
has of course been one of the main stumbling blocks
of theologians, who are obliged to maintain the former as
the basis of individual responsibility and must admit the
latter to be a consequence of an all-powerful God. Sartre
holds individual freedom and responsibility to be a fact,
and finds it impossible to reconcile that fact rationally
with the idea of God.

Assuming the validity of these arguments it might still
be possible to establish the existence of God by criteria
other than rational coherence. In the method of existentialism such coherence is only one aspect of the contact of
the existent individual with the world. According to
Sartre, we know of the existence of the in-itself by intuition and individual experiences such as the feeling
of "anguish" can have ontological significance. What

evidence can we find for the existence of God in our experience?

Sense experience, which reveals to us the in-itself, can give us no clue. Sartre rejects the method of Thomist realism, which ties the world of particulars to universal essences, and he sees the in-itself as identical with appearances, uncreated and purposeless. As for our inner experience, Sartre is no less unequivocal. His first novel, *Nausea*, centers around the metaphysically significant experience which he calls "nausea." The experience of "nausea" is the experience of a world where objects have no role or function, but exist by themselves in a meaningless plenitude. "Every existent is born without reason, remains through weakness and dies by chance." In such a world the idea of God, also, is meaningless.

If the existence of God is ontologically impossible, the undeniable fact of a widespread belief in God remains to be accounted for. In considering this problem Sartre follows Freud and traces belief to its roots in individual psychology. This results in the description of a socially important myth with a relatively permanent basis in human reality.

In order to understand Sartre's description of the sources of religious belief it is necessary to examine the aspect of human reality which he terms "transcendence." This is a characteristic of being-for-itself, and as such, of man, since the for-itself is present in the world as human consciousness. Just as freedom is a reality for man because the for-itself is a nothingness which must deny being-in-itself in order that the world may be revealed, so transcendence is a condition of human existence because the for-itself is a nothingness toward a projected state of itself. In other words, man is incomplete and, at the same time, a desire for his own completion. Completion can mean only the surpassing of the nothingness of consciousness toward what it lacks, which is the factual existence which characterizes being-in-itself. This projected synthesis would be the self-conscious totality of being which we have earlier described as God. We can now understand the sense in which Sartre can say that man fundamentally is the desire to be God.

Since the idea of God is contradictory and therefore impossible, the project of man to be God cannot be realized. If the lack is fulfilled, it ceases to be a lack. Nevertheless, the project of being God remains constitutive of human reality. Man is in a state of tension in relation to his transcendent and impossible goal, which in the present expresses itself as a restlessness or dynamism. This dynamism is directed toward the realization of an ideal self, or the individual as he would be if the goals of his project were realized. This project belongs to what Sartre calls the prereflective or what is commonly referred to as the unconscious level of personality. Further, it is the source of value in the world, the concept of a desirable possible state of things not identical with their present state.

The importance which Sartre gives to the goal-seeking characteristic of man cannot be too strongly emphasized. It would be inadequate to view man as having goals; instead, he appears as a process toward the realization of a goal. As such, he never coincides with himself, but is constantly surpassing himself. This description applies as a part of the human condition, and would be universally applicable save for the possibility of flight from this condition into bad faith, which in this case would involve the denial of transcendence. Sartre is here close to the Thomist view of "human nature," which holds that:

All beings aim at, strive after, desire, their own perfection. But goodness is that which all things aim at, strive after, desire, since the essence of goodness consists in this, that it is in some way desirable. Therefore perfection and whatever leads to it are good. Becoming, the proper condition of all created being, is the way to perfection, to fullness of being.[3]

It should not be concluded, however, that Sartre is in agreement with the Thomists on the question of human nature. The point made here only illustrates that the idea of man in suspense with relation to a valuable end which he is not cannot be considered peculiar to Sartre's ontology.

It is in the fact of human transcendence that we find the first explanation of religion.

Whatever may be the myths and rites of the religion considered, God is first "sensible to the heart" of man as the one who identifies and defines him in his ultimate and fundamental project. If man possesses a pre-ontological comprehension of the being of God, it is not the great wonders of nature nor the power of society which have conferred it upon him. God, value and supreme end of transcendence, represents the permanent limit in terms of which man makes known to himself what he is. To be man means to reach toward being God.[4]

The concept of God inherent in the human experience of transcendence is that of a perfect being, both in wisdom and goodness. But the fact that this concept is a projection of the human condition cannot establish the existence of God, and religious belief remains an illusion.

A second source of religious belief is the experience which we have of other people, or subjects, in society. Sartre points to the existence of other people as the origin of one dimension of human reality, our being-for-others. Since this being-for-others constitutes my objective being in the world it is essential to any project which I might have for myself; that is, self-realization must take its departure from and be achieved by modifications of my objective being. The necessity of achieving my ends through my being as an object for others makes this being valuable to me, and the relationship between the project and being-for-others must be self-respect. This is true, of course, only for the authentic individual, for the essence of bad faith is flight from one or another dimension of human reality; vice, says Sartre, is the love of failure. Failure would be, in this case, the abandonment of the requirement of self-respect and acceptance of a degrading status for my being-for-others.

Because this objective being, however valuable to us, is nevertheless only an object for the other, shame is our normal reaction to the presence of the other. This shame can be avoided, and our self-respect secured, in one type of interpersonal relationship, love. If I am loved, my objective being becomes the choice of the other's freedom, as it must be of my own. In a love relationship I at once realize my object status and feel justified in it, since I represent the highest value for the one I love. Love is then a basic need of personality, although the ideal of love does not necessarily motivate all interpersonal relations, since to satisfy both parties it must be reciprocal and thus tends to be exclusive in nature, and since the need can be suppressed because, for example, of fear of failure. And it can never fully succeed; it would require permanent possession of the other's freedom in order to be secure in the choice of this freedom, and that is in principle impossible. Possession is not love; I require the other to love me voluntarily, by virtue of a constantly renewed free choice, and yet his very freedom makes me insecure.

The experience of love leads us to belief in the existence of an absolute being for whom this problem would be resolved: whose objective being would coincide with the choice of his freedom. This absolute being is God, for whom self-respect is not a demand but an actuality. Once again Sartre finds God to be a symbol for the ideal solution to a human problem which is not, for humans, capable of a solution. In this context it is also clear why God is pictured as demanding love, and loving in return. If Jesus loves me, the failure of more mundane love is easier to bear, or can be avoided altogether by the substitution of divine for mundane love. There remains, however, the problem which apparently was bothering Baudelaire when he referred to God as a prostitute because He loves everybody.

A third suggestion of the existence of God, this time in His character as Creator, comes to us through our experience of the world, which in all its parts appears to possess the qualities of potentiality and instrumentality. A world where everything has a purpose is an ordered world. As a watch requires a watchmaker, so an ordered world requires a Creator.

Sartre agrees with Catholic philosophers that the world appears to man as constituting both a factual and moral order. He rejects, however, the Catholic explanation of this fact, which is in terms of the ordering of the world by God and its resulting accessibility to rational beings who are made in the image of God. Because men are the children of God they are able to understand His creations. Sartre explains the natural order, however, as a product of human transcendence. Because my prerational project of myself is implicit in all my perceptions, it causes me to see the world as organized by my purposes. Objects take on the characteristics of aids or hindrances in the pursuit of my projects. The purposes which organize the world, even giving a function to such natural occurrences as the rains of spring, are not the purposes of God but those of the individual. These purposes, of course, represent a certain organization and modification of the standards accepted by the group to which the individual belongs, so that a degree of unity will prevail in the world outlook of any particular group. What is taken for an objective world order guaranteed by God is actually the product of many individual projects.

Finally, we are led to postulate the existence of God by our experience of being an "us-object." This experience occurs when a group identifies itself as such in relation to another group or person who looks at them as objects. A number of persons see themselves as forming a definite group or community when they find themselves so classed in the view of a third party. If the third party is a foreigner, the reaction is a consciousness of nationality. Similarly, the presence of the bourgeois is required for the class solidarity of the proletariat. The experience of solidarity with a particular group implies the possibility of a similar solidarity with all mankind.

This effort at recovering the human totality can not take place without positing the existence of a Third, who is on principle distinct from humanity and in whose eyes humanity is wholly object. . . . This concept is the same as that of the being-who-looks-at and who can never be looked-at; that is, it is one with the idea of God. . . . Thus the limiting-concept of humanity . . . and the limiting-concept of God imply one another and are correlative.[5]

These, then, are the four basic aspects of human experience which lead us to a belief in the existence of God. First there is God as the individual self writ large in the heavens. This God is perfection and goodness, the object of the most profound desire of human consciousness. The second is God as the other consciousness, which can justify us by making our being the absolute choice of its freedom. The third is God the Creator, source of meaning in the universe. And the fourth is God as the absolute third, the Other who sees humanity as human kind. While the first three experiences find God in aspects of our own transcendence, the last is an experience of being an object for the transcendence of another. ". . . the Us-object precipitates us into the world; we experience it in shame as a community alienation." [6] Here we have God as King, or Lord and Master. He is an anthropomorphic God Who demands obedience.

The fact of religion then is not an anomaly explicable as the vestigial superstition of a bygone age but rather reflects permanent and basic aspects of the human condition. Nevertheless, the central concept of religion, the existence of God, is an illusion. Thus, a belief in God is unjustifiable and unnecessary. In order to show that Sartre considers such a belief to be in fact detrimental to human welfare it will be necessary to examine the "religious personality" as he sees it, as well as the function which he gives to religion in the social order.

Sartre's analysis of religious belief in the individual shows such belief to be a form of "bad faith," or refusal to face the fact of human freedom. Bad faith is a response to a situation in which man faces the difficulty of conquering himself as a self in spite of his personal suffering and the dead weight of his past. The child is born into

a world created by others, but which he, by virtue of the
necessity of his dependence, accepts as his own. His
progress to maturity requires that he reject the authority
of his parents as a justification for his view of the world
and assert, in his turn, the world as it appears to him.
Then each man must carve a slow and painful path
through achievement and frustration toward a transcendent perfection which he will never reach. The
recognition of solitude is accompanied by nausea, and
the recognition of freedom, which opens the gate to the
future, is inseparable from anguish. The concomitant of
desire is frustration, and the ultimate satisfaction of desire impossible. It is the "human condition" with its inner conflict and struggle which leads to "bad faith."

Sartre's discussion of bad faith begins with an examination of the lie. In order to lie one must know what is true
and then determine to conceal it. Bad faith resembles a
lie in that ". . . the one who practices bad faith is hiding
a displeasing truth or presenting as truth a pleasing un-
truth." [7] It differs from a lie in that bad faith is comparable to a lie to oneself. An ordinary lie has the purpose of creating a certain impression in another, of de-
ceiving the other person. Bad faith may also arise out of
relations with other persons, but when a liar believes his
own lie, he is in bad faith.

Sartre gives us an example of bad faith in the attitudes
and behavior of a flirtatious woman.[8] Going out for the
first time with a certain man, she requires that he be
interested in her body and because of his advances must
be aware that he in fact is. Yet she is not willing to be
considered as a sexual object. "She is profoundly aware
of the desire which she inspires, but the desire cruel and
naked would humiliate and horrify her." So she refuses
to take cognizance of this desire, and while not making

any gesture that would irretrievably alienate her ad-
mirer, interprets his attentions as directed solely toward
her transcendence. "She draws her companion up to the
most lofty regions of sentimental speculation; she speaks
of Life, of her life, she shows herself in her essential
aspect—a personality, a consciousness."

Freudian psychology might explain this behavior in
terms of repression. Her behavior is motivated by sexual
desire, but this desire is kept out of the ego by the superego, or censor. The superego suppresses a desire which
conflicts with socially acceptable behavior and the ego
is conscious only of approved motivations. Sartre rejects
this explanation, arguing that the censor could not suppress a motive without being aware of it. He finds a
better explanation in the concept of bad faith, in spite
of the difficulty involved in postulating two contradictory beliefs within the same consciousness. Bad faith is
possible because of the ambiguous nature of human
personality. Our body, our actions, and our history are
being-in-itself, while our consciousness is being-for-itself
and as such freedom and a flight toward transcendence.
This enables us to make use of the dualities involved in
the fact that we cannot be completely identified with our
behavior at any given moment, that our being as seen by
ourselves differs from our being as seen by others, and
that our history or past actions cannot determine our
future being. In short, as Sartre puts it, "we have to deal
with human reality as a being which is what it is not and
which is not what it is." Thus, even good faith, in the
sense that I am what I am, is impossible. Or better, it is
bad faith. Sincerity is only possible when it asserts that
I have been this and I can be otherwise.

Returning to Sartre's example, we see that the woman
is in bad faith because she identifies herself with her

transcendence at the expense of her being-for-others. She lies to herself. Her bad faith is unstable, in constant danger of becoming a rejection of all unacceptable advances on the one hand or a complete acceptance of the man's degrading aims on the other.

> . . . bad faith . . . vacillates continually between good faith and cynicism. . . . it presents nonetheless an autonomous and durable form. It can even be the normal aspect of life for a very great number of people.[9]

Among these people we will find many, if not all, persons who make religious faith an important part of their lives.

One form of religious belief in bad faith is that which Sartre finds in Baudelaire during his periods of faith in God. It is an attempt to avoid the recognition of one's own existence by belief in a God Who guarantees order in the universe. Baudelaire chose to be evil, and as this is impossible except within a pre-established framework of good and evil, he sought in God the source of this order. The nature of Baudelaire's view of God is well illustrated by this passage from *My Heart Laid Bare:*

> *Calculation in favor of God.*
> Nothing exists without a purpose.
> Thus my existence has a purpose. What purpose? I don't know.
> It is thus not I that have chosen it.
> It is thus someone wiser than I.
> I must pray this someone to enlighten me. It is the wisest thing.[10]

From this it is clear that Baudelaire was unwilling to consider that his existence was absurd and that he must find his own purpose. And this denial of his freedom led him directly to the existence of God. Baudelaire prefers the moderate anguish of defying an established God to the recognition of his own responsible freedom. Another will exalt duty and obedience to God for the same reason. In this case the fear of failing God substitutes itself for the anguish of freedom. Both are in bad faith, because their flight from freedom is only possible because they are conscious of their freedom. Baudelaire "saw that he was incomparable, incommunicable, uncreated, absurd, useless, abandoned in the most complete isolation, . . ." [11] This in bad faith can lead to a belief in God where "what counted therefore even more than the mere existence of this all-powerful being was his nature and functions. Now it must be noticed that Baudelaire's God was a God of terror. . . . Christ seems to have been unknown to Baudelaire . . ." [12]

This type of God-oriented bad faith seems to be identical with the religion of the "authoritarian character" of Erich Fromm.

. . . the "will of the Lord," . . . for the authoritarian character . . . is always a higher power outside of the individual, toward which the individual can do nothing but submit. The authoritarian character worships the past. What has been, will eternally be. . . . Whoever has once sinned is chained eternally to his sin with iron shackles.[13]

As Fromm found this type of character to have a definite political bias, so Sartre finds a definite political attitude to be typical of this type of religious mind. When Baudelaire looks at politics, he takes as his guide:

. . . Joseph de Maistre, the final incarnation of the *Other*. "It was he," said Baudelaire, "who taught me to think." In order to feel completely at his ease, ought he not to occupy a specially designated place in the natural and social hierarchy? The austere thinker who was in bad faith taught him the intoxicating arguments of conservatism. . . . "In politics, the true saint is the man who uses his whip and kills the people for their own good."

That, no doubt, was written with a shiver of pleasure. . . .
What security, since the victim was forbidden to decide on
it [his own good] and since in the throes of his sufferings he
was told that it was for *his* Good . . . that he was dying! It
was also necessary that this very strict hierarchy should be
pre-established and that the men with whips should make
themselves its guardians.[14]

Sartre carries through his analysis with other tools than
Fromm, and it is interesting to note that while *Escape
from Freedom* was published in the U.S. in 1941, the
discussion of bad faith appeared in *Being and Nothingness* in the Paris of 1943 under German occupation.

We find another example of religious bad faith in
the conversion of Daniel, a character in Sartre's unfinished
series of novels entitled *Roads to Freedom*. Daniel is a
homosexual who feels with shame the gulf between an
invert and respectable society. He seeks relief from his
inner torment in the look of others who know him for
what he is, contemptible. In the company of the other
who knows his secret his character is fixed and, hateful
though he finds himself, he is no longer freely responsible
for his nature. His homosexual image is his reality for
the other, and since he cannot escape his desires he
wants simply to *be*, without recourse, that image. In
order to do so, he attempts to smother his transcendence
by being a homosexual as a rock is a rock, in the realm
of being-in-itself:

To be stone, motionless, without feeling . . . blind and deaf,
. . . perhaps I would manage to be myself. . . . To be myself, a pederast, wicked, a coward, . . . To be a pederast, as
the oak is oak. To be extinguished. To put out the inner eye.[15]

But the company of such another was impossible; the
demands of society prevented him from making himself
known, for example to his wife, and no human could be

constant enough or close enough to know him in all his
depravity. This problem is solved by a religious conversion.

He was the object of a look. A look which searched him to his
depths, . . . and which was not his look; . . . condemned
him to be himself, coward, hypocrite, pederast for eternity.[16]

Shall I call it God? He was not astonished, he thought: that
had to come. Sooner or later. I was sure that there was something.[17]

This conversion is achieved by his entry into the Church.

Daniel: I went to see the priest. Father, I said to him, . . .
           does your religion teach that God sees us?
Priest: He sees us, . . . he reads our hearts.
Daniel: But what does he see there?
Priest: God sees everything.[18]

Daniel denies his freedom by calling on God to guarantee
that he is an object, his being-for-others. This is necessary because he has felt in anguish his freedom and responsibility for himself and wishes to escape from it.

As for his political views, it would appear that Daniel
was essentially nonpolitical. Primarily concerned with a
static personal solution to a personal problem, he sees
political events as marginal and unimportant. But as he
watches the entry of the German army into Paris, he
takes pleasure in the downfall of the society which made
him guilty. His resignation before the established order
of things is replaced by a pleasurable appreciation of
the political victory of the forces of evil.

. . . he thought: "Our conquerors!" and he was filled with
pleasure. . . . it was the victory of contempt, of violence and
of bad faith, it was the victory of the Earth.[19]

Bad faith has given way to cynicism, and he returns to
his homosexual practices. Thus we have a picture of a

political cipher, who in a period of crisis and change
slides into nihilism. Religious faith for him has been an
escape from the problems involved in living in the
world.

These examples of religious belief as a form of bad
faith represent two of the most extensive studies by
Sartre of the nature of religious belief. Such belief was
in Baudelaire a form of the "seriousness" which gives man
a ready-made place in the world. Its political corollary
was the need for an authoritarian political regime. Religious belief for Daniel is a form of the "God-Gaze," or
escape from the inner life by immersion in our being-
for-others. It carries with it resignation before the
political status quo and a subterranean political nihilism.

Turning to Sartre's view of the social and political
function of institutionalized religion we find that it is
congruent with his description of individual religious experience. As God is the ally of Daniel in his attempt to
smother his freedom, so Jupiter in *The Flies* appears as
the ally of a tyrant who fears the freedom of others:

Jupiter.— . . . the same secret weighs heavily on our
hearts.

Égisthe.—I have no secret.

Jupiter.—Yes. The same as I. The unhappy secret of Gods
and kings: it is that men are free. They are free, Égisthe.
You know it, and they don't know it.

Égisthe.—Heavens, if they knew it they would set fire to
the four corners of my palace. For fifteen years I have put
on an act to hide their power from them. . . . who am I, if
not the fear that the others have of me?

Jupiter.— . . . For a hundred thousand years I have
danced before men. . . . They have to watch me: as long as
they have their eyes fixed on me, they forget to look into
themselves.[20]

In this passage Sartre asserts a relationship between passive acceptance of religion and political authority. Religion functions, as Marx contended, as the opium of the people. By turning their attention away from the actual facts of their experience to mythical duties and rewards, it prevents them from realizing their power to deal directly and personally with the problems which face them.

I have attempted to illustrate Sartre's views on the existence of God, the sources of the concept of God in human experience, and the nature and function of religious belief from the personal and social points of view. The God whose existence is denied by Sartre is that of Catholic philosophy in the tradition of St. Thomas Aquinas. There is little in his writings to indicate what his position would be with respect to another theology, for example one which affirms the concept of God as a meaningful symbol with roots in human reality. In fact, Sartre does not so much deny the existence of God as assert that philosophy can have no knowledge of His existence. It is also not clear that Sartre considers all religious belief to be in bad faith; he has in fact indicated that the choice of a religious vocation can be "wise." [21] What can be concluded from his examples is that he considers religious belief in its most prevalent present form to be in bad faith. The validity of these positions will be examined in the following chapter, which deals with the consequences Sartre draws from the absence of God.

Sartre and Catholic Man

CHAPTER VI

Since Sartre describes his position as "nothing else than an attempt to draw all the consequences of a coherent atheistic position," a consideration of his disagreements with the Catholic view of man should further clarify the nature of Sartrean existentialism. Sartre has frequently criticized points of Catholic social doctrine, and identifies himself with the secular tradition of the French left, of which his philosophy might be considered a reformulation. The Catholic doctrine which he criticizes is that commonly referred to as Thomism because of its origins in the philosophy of St. Thomas Aquinas. There have been of course Catholic philosophers who, to a greater or lesser extent, disagreed with Thomist doctrines. Nevertheless, Thomism is unquestionably the dominant tradition in Catholic thought.

The existence of God is the basic presupposition upon which the Thomist view of the world depends. Nature is viewed as an ordered hierarchy with man at its summit, in which every existent has a role suited to its capacities. God is both the origin and the end of this planned and purposeful world. The order of the world is guaranteed by natural laws, whose authority is derived from the fact that they are commanded by God. Aquinas followed Aristotle in contending that the laws of nature are accessible to human reason, so that man can know the world as it really is. Once a natural law has become known it is not subject to dispute, and is universal in its application. The content of natural law is descriptive not only of what are commonly termed facts but also of the ends or purposes which God has assigned to everything in nature. In short, God has made the world and, as the highest of his creations, man, who being made in the image of God, is capable of understanding all of creation. The instrument of this understanding, one might say the divine in man, is reason. Of course, this does not mean that all is known to man, or that reasoning cannot err. Man cannot see everything, as God does, but within the domain of his experience and through right reason he can attain objective certainty.

Since the existence of God is impossible for Sartre, he rejects the idea of an objective world order subject to universal laws which are accessible to human reason. Being-in-itself is intuited directly, but is without potentiality or purpose, and consequently refers to nothing beyond itself. We have here perhaps the fundamental insight of existentialism, namely, that the world in which man finds himself is contingent, gratuitous, and meaningless. This gratuitousness enters human experience only in the experience of nausea, and normally the world appears to be in order. But we have already seen that order is projected by man into the world, and is not guaranteed by a God. Consequently, the natural laws which we find in the world are relative to the perspective of particular men, societies, and periods in history. Natural laws are not descriptive of being, and thus can be neither universal nor permanent.

With respect to the concept of natural law, it would seem that in Sartre's philosophy man himself has become

God. In the normal course of life for the existing individual the world is ordered and purposeful. Reality can therefore be described in terms of natural laws, which govern its organization and events. The world would thus appear to man much as the Thomists describe it, except for the fact that the world shares the contingency of the human individual: unlike God, men are isolated, plural, and temporary sources of a world. The result is a marked change in the relation of man to the world; no longer a secure home, the world has become a project of the individual for which he is responsible.

The Catholic concept of human nature assigns a permanent and universal essence to man, discoverable by rational intuition and taking the form of a definition of man. Man's essence, rationally determinable character, or human nature is that of a rational, free, and social being. Because of his rational nature he can know himself, and his place in the natural order. One of the things which he knows about himself is his natural or God-given end, which is the pursuit of happiness. The pursuit of happiness has a definite meaning in Catholic philosophy, and should not be confused with pleasure, or the satisfaction of recurring desires. Instead, happiness lies in virtue, and the goal of happiness is the goal of complete goodness, which is true only of God. Catholic man is thus characterized by striving, a striving to be God. This is not primarily a statement of obligation, assigning a duty to man, but rather a description of the way all men in fact are, of human being. Because man is free, however, he may deviate from his basic task of achieving God. When he does so, he is leaving the realm of the natural and entering that of nothingness. Only action in accordance with nature can be meaningful for man. Finally, the inclusion of the term social in the Catholic definition of man means that, as Aristotle said, the individual realizes his full potentiality or develops himself only in a social context.

Sartre does not accept rational intuition as a method, because his philosophy excludes the possibility of a correspondence between human reason and an objective order of things independent of man. Also, he holds that a definition of man is impossible, and dissociates himself from the view that there is any permanent and universal human nature. Nevertheless, he asserts that there is a permanent and universal human condition, which some have thought to be suspiciously close to a concept of human nature. If, for the time being, we accept it as such, then it would appear that Sartre's human condition is very close to the Catholic concept of human nature as summarized above, both in form and content. The Catholics ascribe an emotional nature to man, which he shares with other animals, and a rational nature, which is distinctively human. Sartre has written nothing about animals, which is considered by some to be a major shortcoming of his philosophy. As far as humans are concerned, he also distinguishes what might be described as rational and emotional levels, the reflective *cogito* and the prereflective *cogito*. Sartre describes man as a striving toward the realization of God; so do the Catholics. Finally, the social nature of man has its counterpart in Sartre's being-for-others, which ties man to other individuals and the groups to which he belongs. Both assert the freedom of man as a basic constituent of his being. Hardly anyone would deny that, in some sense, man is rational and social. There are those who assert that the statement "man is free" is a meaningless proposition, and deny that man can be characterized as having one fundamental desire or goal, or that this goal is to "be God" in any sense. It is particularly on the subject of freedom and transcendence that Sartre and the Catholics would seem to have more in common than either would have with some other contemporary philosophical viewpoints.

Sartre's psychology is, however, much more complex and closer to modern views than that of the Catholics. The goal-seeking level of consciousness is not the reflective but the prereflective level, and reflection is not the guide but usually the servant of deeper motivations. If we search for an analogy here in Catholic doctrine, it would be necessary to go back to St. Augustine rather than to the Thomists. Similarly, man is not simply "social" for Sartre; a discussion of being-for-others would necessitate a too lengthy digression at this point, but it can be said that this tie with society is as much a threat to the individual as it is a condition for his development. Catholic doctrine views the individual as having ready-made tendencies, which he has only to realize, while Sartre sees man as a problem to which there can only be individual solutions. It is for this reason that Sartre denies that he has developed a doctrine of human nature:

> Atheistic existentialism . . . states that if God does not exist, there is at least one being in whom existence precedes essence, a being who exists before he can be defined by any concept, and that this being is man, . . . there is no human nature, since there is no God to conceive it.[1]

Man's nature is what he is, and he is what he has made of himself in his individual existence. I am not human nature, but a particular response to the human condition. This implies a radical difference between the Sartrean and Catholic concepts of human freedom. For the Catholics, man must choose whether or not to realize a given essential nature. Sartrean man invents his own essence.

The third point of difference between Sartre and the Thomists is in the field of ethics. The natural order is a moral order for Catholic man because he is free, and may by his own choice persist in or abandon the pursuit of virtue. Because of this freedom his relation to his appointed end is one of obligation and not of necessity. Should he choose to realize his essence, however, his path is laid out for him. The natural law prescribes, in the case of man, the necessary steps toward eternal happiness in the knowledge of God. In other words, natural law becomes a series of moral commands which are universally obligatory. Since the circumstances accompanying an action are a controlling factor in the moral quality of that action, good behavior will vary between societies and from one period in history to another. But the supreme end of man and the basic principles of moral conduct apply everywhere. The rightness of particular actions is thus subject to rational determination, and involves merely the application of known universals—such as the preservation of life, the propagation of the species, etc.—to empirically determined situations. Reason, because of its correspondence with the natural order of God, furnishes an objective standard of right behavior.

In accordance with this view of ethics, Catholic moralists put a great deal of emphasis on habit and early training as means toward the establishment of patterns of good behavior. The requirements of the natural moral law being known—and proclaimed as such by the Catholic church—it seems logical to take advantage of the human tendency toward persisting in familiar patterns of behavior by giving right action the prestige of the status quo. The content of Catholic moral law is quite detailed, including such well known proscriptions as those of abortion, divorce, and birth control. Persistence in habits of good behavior is termed virtue, and virtually all Catholics are acquainted with the standard catalogue of virtues.

Sartre's ethics resembles that of the Catholics insofar as living according to one's nature and facing honestly the human condition both involve an acceptance of the conditions of human being. Apart from this similarity, the basic differences are clearly consequences of Sartre's denial of the existence of God. Without a natural order within which all men find themselves, there would seem to be no definite limit to the variation in circumstances which provide the context for moral actions, so that the search for universally valid ethical principles even of an ultimate nature would seem to be fruitless. Also, the achievement of the standpoint of God as the ultimate moral goal, impossible in any complete sense for both Sartre and the Catholics, is only the meaning of the individual's project, and not its content. That is, the actual projects of individuals differ, and the values determined by the projects also differ. Human beings are thus characterized not by the unanimous search for a morally desirable goal, but by disparate goals and diverse value orientations. Finally, since being-for-others is, so to speak, the outside of the individual which must be changed for moral improvement to be realized, personal virtue is intimately involved with changes in the social order. Morality requires not conformity to the natural but creation of the artificial. In short, Sartre abandons the notion of a rationally intelligible human type which can serve as the standard for all men.

The climate of Sartre's ethics is quite different from that of Catholic Thomism, although it bears some similarity to that of Catholic writers such as Bernanos and Graham Greene. Since the rightness of a particular action cannot be guaranteed in advance, but remains always in question, and because the individual is responsible for his actions, the motive presiding over the decision to act and the consequences of the action acquire an agonizing importance. Instead of asking what I must do, the moral problem becomes what I really want to do and how my decision will affect my own future and that of others. In a sense, Sartre contends that I will always act rightly, since the standard of right is my own project which determines my emotions as well as my reasonings. This, however, is only true for the authentic individual, and even he is constantly tempted by the desire to conform to exterior standards of right. This is the temptation of bad faith, which offers an escape from responsibility for personal decision in the light of what I know and feel about myself. Its mechanisms are the falsification of reality, rationalization, and repression. Authenticity requires a willingness to face the necessity of a decision, the recognition of its moral aspects, and the acceptance of responsibility for it. In this context, habit appears as a threat to virtue, because it tends to result in behavior unsuited to new situations. Training, however necessary for children, is a restriction of another's freedom. Sartre refuses to give advice as to the proper moral course for a young man faced with a decision; [2] it is possible to give information on the conditions of moral decision, but no one person can tell another what his values should be. As for the moral claims of Catholicism, Sartre declares that we live in a period of mystifications, that the social order in France rests upon them, and that Catholicism is one of them. [3] The task of the existentialist writer is that of recalling the individual to his real problems in order that he may deal with them in a responsible fashion.

Sartre's position on the Catholic moral law has much in common with that of modern positivists. He regards statements of value as meaningful only in terms of a subjective commitment by an individual to a particular situation as valuable and not as descriptions of an objective reality. However, he also objects to Catholic ethics on moral grounds, and it is this moral concern which leads him to say that he finds it to be "very distressing that God does not exist, . . ." [4] Distressing because, without God, man cannot be justified but must justify himself. When Sartre rejects the Christian legal heritage, in spite of its value as a standard for social justice, he does so in order to assert a type of moral evaluation which is more consistent with the empiricism and relativism that characterize the social sciences.

We have seen Sartre deny the existence of God on grounds of rationality and human experience. We have then seen him explain the existence of religion as a naturalistic phenomenon rooted as an illusion in certain basic aspects of human psychology. Next we have shown that Sartre views religious belief, at least in some of its most important forms, as a variety of bad faith. This bad faith involves a denial by the individual of his freedom and is accompanied by political attitudes inconsistent with the principles of a free society. Because of its short-term interest in securing conformity on whatever grounds, government tends to encourage this belief and these attitudes. Sartre's atheistic position was then shown to include a rejection of the concepts of human nature and natural law. Finally, we have seen that Sartre attacks Catholic ethics as authoritarian and legalistic.

Many Catholics have taken on the burden of answering Sartre, partly because of the challenge he presents to French Catholicism and partly within the context of a more general attempt to reconcile what they regard as the insights of existentialism with the traditional Catholic philosophy of Thomism. The comments of some of their spokesmen include the following points. There is a basically religious concern in Sartre's existentialism, and the return of this emphasis to the forefront in modern thought is a healthy sign. More particularly, the Sartrean emphasis on the priority of existence over essence is valuable in that it corrects the stultifying essentialism of the idealists, some of which had crept into Catholic thought. The influence of the idealists on Catholic doctrine took the form of insisting on the prior reality of such essences as human nature, and deducing from the essence of man the most minute characteristics of human behavior, into which the individual was left to fit himself as best he could. Existentialism counteracts this with an emphasis upon regarding human nature as not simply an idea in the mind of God, but as a description of actually existing men. But, according to Maritain, the first existentialist was St. Thomas Aquinas, if not Aristotle, and Sartre's comparative position is weak because he overlooks entirely the fact of rational intuition of essences:

. . . the differences in metaphysical point of view, profound though they be, will nevertheless not preclude certain contacts between this [Thomistic] existentialism and contemporary existentialism. . . . If all this were not spoiled by the acceptance of absurdity and by the eviction of nature and the *forma rationis,* . . .[5]

Another Catholic philosopher attempts to save essentialism by denying abstract reality to essences, which exist only insofar as they are embodied in a particular existent, and by multiplying their number and increasing the complexity of their relationships. A single existent might have two contradictory essences, as contradiction in human reason does not mean an impossibility for the will of God. One could say that Sartre has the defects of his virtues—if St. Thomas had not supplied us with a philosophy which possesses the same virtues without the defects.

As for Sartre's atheism, it is presented as an act of faith. "It is not useless to remark that atheistic existentialism itself remains dependent upon theology, though an inverted theology. For it, as for Marxism, atheism is a *point of departure* accepted in advance." [6] This original position, adopted in advance, prevents Sartre from following through his own deeply religious philosophy to its existential consequences. He has avoided embarrassing questions about the existence of God by relegating metaphysics, which tries to give a causal explanation of the world, to the status of hypotheses as opposed to the certainty of ontology. His arguments against the existence of God are ". . . just as strong and just as weak as Sartre's general ontology. . . . He defines being in-itself in a univocal and material way and then shows that being, as so defined, excludes consciousness and the other attributes usually applied to God. Clearly enough, the trouble lies in the doctrine of the In-itself . . ." [7]

In the defense of Catholic ethics against Sartre's attacks there is a great deal of emphasis on what might be called Catholicism for the elite. Gilson contends that all the essences of human nature may never be known, and certainly are not known now. Maritain points out that the actions of Saints are rationally inexplicable, but nevertheless on a higher plane than the good for ordinary human nature:

St. Thomas teaches that the standard of the gifts of the Holy Ghost is higher than that of the moral virtues; that of the gift of counsel is higher than that of prudence. The Saints always amaze us. . . . They have their own kind of mean, their own kinds of standards. But they are valid only for each one of them. . . . their standards are higher than those of reason, . . .[8]

He also insists that no action can be good unless fully understood and willed as such by the particular individual. Although it is correct to say that there are objective moral rules and duties, mere compliance with them does not make individual behavior good. Obedience to a rule must be a spontaneous expression of the individual's actual desire and will before the action can be called virtuous. In short, Sartre is attacking a straw man, and Catholic doctrine is global enough to include his "atheistic" insights.

Finally, the criticism is turned on Sartre's picture of man. According to Sartre's doctrine, man is basically the desire to be God, and this desire is incapable of fulfillment. If human perfection is also ruled out by Catholic doctrine, progress is possible and in addition man can hope for grace. Thus Sartre is accused of pessimism. But Sartre denies this accusation. And, on this point, Maritain agrees with him. "Manage at all costs to make atheism livable. But what if by chance that could not be managed? What if by chance a man could not get along, or adapt himself? The question does not even arise. It is deliberately suppressed and forbidden. M. Sartre is right in declaring himself firmly optimistic and in leaving the tragic sense to Christians . . ."[9]

Those Catholics who trace Sartre's atheism to his concept of the in-itself, which stresses the absurdity of being and rules out any idea of a natural order independent of man, are partially correct. The conception of a universe lacking in rationality or purpose is not, however, peculiar to Sartre. It is characteristic of all existentialists, some of whom are religious thinkers. Where this sense of estrangement between man and things does not lead to atheism, it leads to an emphasis on the distance between man and God, and the inscrutability of the divine plan. Gilson himself reflects this aspect of existentialism when he describes the limitations of reason for defining human nature. The most fundamental reason for Sartre's atheism would thus seem to be implied by his refusal to go beyond the hypothetical in his metaphysics, and by his reluctance to center his philosophy on a concept which goes beyond the testimony of experience. The spirit of science is opposed to the *credo quia absurdum est,* and science refuses to speculate about first causes; so does Sartre. His atheism does not result from a belief accepted in advance, but rather from a lack of belief. Those who must believe, and those who do not share Sartre's humility before exposition of the supernatural, will not be satisfied with his position on this issue. Nevertheless, it is worth something to have a naturalistic philosophy which includes the moral and spiritual insights once thought to be identified with religion.

Competent Catholic philosophers can point successfully to aspects of their doctrine which are inconsistent with the picture that Sartre presents of Catholicism. It should not be quickly concluded, however, that his criticisms are for this reason unjustified. No one could hope to consider all the views which have been advanced in the name of Catholicism, many of which are contradictory. It should be enough if Sartre directs his remarks to a position that is of major importance in the Catholic tradition and has frequently received the approval of the Church.

As for the practical implications of Catholic doctrine

for the lives of its adherents, it is worth noting that
Sartre's view of Catholic social doctrine is supported by
others who, while influenced by existentialists, have
never been referred to as nihilists. In this category can be
included prominent theologians of the Protestant faith.
Like Sartre, these writers find a strong tendency in traditional religion toward what Paul Tillich calls "heteron-
omy." This is a state of affairs in which man is under the
tyranny of an alien law, which is destructive of personality and ethical life. Catholic ethics is considered to be an
example of such an alien law. The combination of natural
law and ecclesiastical authority produces an exterior and
rigid legalism. According to Reinhold Niebuhr:

> The whole concept of natural law rests upon a Stoic-Aristo-
> telian rationalism which assumes fixed historical structures
> and norms which do not in fact exist. . . . The moral cer-
> tainties of natural law in Catholic thought are all dubious.
> . . . The more specific they become the more they are sus-
> pect as "self-evident" propositions of the natural law.[10]

Catholicism in the general emphasis of its theory and
practice would seem to risk falling into Tillich's category
of systems which subject ". . . the form and laws of
thinking and acting to authoritative criteria of an ecclesiastical religion or a political quasi-religion, even at
the price of destroying the structures of [individual]
rationality." [11] Sartre might reply to Maritain that the
moral criteria for Saints are of little help to the existing
individual because the Church does not recognize Saints
until after they are dead.

Another writer, this time a social psychologist, whose
views seem to support those of Sartre is Erich Fromm.
Fromm distinguishes between two types of religion:
anthropomorphism, or God as the other person, and
monotheism, which involves an indefinable God-principle

and moral activism. Sartre's analysis of religious belief
in bad faith is close to Fromm's view of anthropomorphism, as was indicated in the example of Baudelaire.
Monotheism as a type of religious belief envisions God
not as an outside power to be obeyed, but rather as a
symbol for human moral achievement. The task of the
believer is not conformity to law but actualization of an
inner God-principle. As for the religion of contemporary
Western society, he contends that:

> . . . in the infantile dependence on an anthropomorphic
> picture of God without the transformation of life according
> to the principles of God, we are closer to a primitive idolatric
> tribe than to the religious culture of the Middle Ages.[12]

Fromm's observations, of course, are meant to apply to
Protestants as well as to Catholics.

It might be contended that there have never been
more than a few truly religious people in Fromm's understanding of monotheism. Sartre's ethics of authenticity,
which provides for a way of life similar to Fromm's
monotheism, would then seem to be essentially an alternative for the elite. It seems, however, that whatever the
advantages of a dogmatic ethics, it is relatively ill-suited
to a period characterized by unprecedented and far-
reaching changes in the manner of life of the average
person, together with a widespread awareness of the
relativity of value judgments. To an important degree,
the moral uncertainties which formerly plagued only the
elite now characterize the majority.

Liberalism as Conservatism

CHAPTER VII

There has been no organizational "Nihil Obstat" to preserve the purity of the liberal doctrine, and as a result
the liberal tradition is compounded of varying philosophical tendencies. What gives liberalism its unity is its
adherence to certain basic themes rather than loyalty
to a particular philosophic system. Nevertheless, much of
its persuasiveness stems from the plausibility of the
philosophic systems with which it has from time to time
allied itself. Sartre criticizes what he considers to be the
three main schools of liberal thought: natural rights philosophy, which was given its most influential statement
by John Locke and flourished in eighteenth-century
France; utilitarianism, which was dominant in the middle
of the nineteenth century; and liberal idealism. The resulting evaluation of liberalism as a contemporary ideology concerns the validity of its underlying philosophical viewpoints and the adequacy of its basic themes to
the requirements of the individual-in-situation in modern
society.

Early liberalism carries on the rationalist tradition of
Catholicism, while rejecting its supernaturalism. The
political theory of John Locke has been described as an
attempt "to defend the rational purpose of government,
. . . against the defense of government as myth, mysti-

cism, and mystery. . . ." [1] The method by which Locke sought to determine the rational purpose of government was analytical; by breaking down the community into its component parts and determining their nature he sought to establish the conditions under which they would unite, and thus to discover the purpose of government. The natural law of which Locke speaks resembles that of Catholicism in that it is subject to rational determination, but differs in taking the form of individual rights rather than rules governing a well-ordered community. "The state of nature has a law of nature to govern it which obliges everyone; and reason, which is that law, teaches all mankind who will but consult it that, being all equal and independent, no one ought to harm another in his life, health, liberty, or possessions; . . ." [2] The doctrine of inherent individual rights prescribed by a natural moral law and functioning as a moral standard for community organization reflects a concern for the social importance of the individual which continued to be characteristic of later formulations of liberalism.

Sartre's objections to the notion of a world well-ordered by the decree of a God-creator have been noted in connection with his criticism of Catholic doctrine. The Sartrean world as revealed in the experience of nausea, in which objects have no order or purpose, is also inconsistent with any notion of a natural order supposedly revealed by science or nontheistic philosophy. In the essay *The Myth of Sisyphus* Camus uses the term "absurd" to describe the relation of man to the world. Far from being a bridge to the world, reason sets man apart from it. Sartre says of Camus' view:

. . . as for the doubts which he raises about the ability of reason, they are in the most recent tradition of French epistemology. When one thinks of scientific nominalism . . . one

will understand better the reproach which our author ad-
dresses to modern science: ". . . you speak to me of an in-
visible planetary system where electrons gravitate around a
nucleus. You explain to me this world with an image. I recognize then that you have resorted to poetry . . ." [3]

Whether termed poetry or hypotheses, the doctrines of
modern science—in spite of their utility—can give us no
more secure "truths" about a natural order than the
theologically oriented doctrines which they have replaced. For Sartre, scientific knowledge is a function of
the purposes of men, not vice versa.

Not that Sartre denies the reality of the world, or the
value of science. What he rejects is the view that nature
can supply moral guidance to man. Sartre's description
of the gulf between man and nature in the novel *Nausea*
is generally invoked as evidence that he has a more
hostile attitude toward it than would appear to be the
case on the basis of his work as a whole. In the novel
he is concerned with describing the experience in which
the individual discovers the absurdity of the world.
Nature seen through the eyes of Rocquentin in his periods of nausea is formless, threatening, and repulsive. On
the other hand, in describing certain forms of bad faith,
Sartre depicts the inertia and objectivity of being-in-itself
as exerting a powerful attraction on the individual. To
the authentic individual nature shows still another face.
Sartre describes New York as "a colonial city, a camp-
ground," [4] where, as in other American cities, one feels
not so much the presence of man as the ubiquity of
nature: "all the hostility, all the cruelty of Nature are
present in this city, . . ." Nevertheless, "I like New York.
. . . This delicate city, ephemeral, which seems each
morning and evening, under the curious rays of the sun,
the simple juxtaposition of rectangular boxes, never op-

presses or depresses. Here one can know the anguish of solitude, not that of oppression." If nature bears a certain amount of impersonality and hostility, it also and by the very fact of its rawness presents the challenge of opportunity: "nowhere do I feel more free . . ." This view of nature still contrasts markedly with that of early liberalism, and throws into relief the degree to which the natural law philosophy depended on the traditional God-centered view of the world.

Sartre declares himself to be "strongly opposed to a certain kind of secular ethics which would like to abolish God with the least possible expense." [5] Liberals abolish God, or at any rate, refuse to accept revelation as the basis of ethics, and yet continue to talk about nature and the natural as a standard for behavior. In like manner, they omit to defend the view that man is made in God's image insofar as both God and man are rational, and continue to assert that reason is a source of ultimate moral values. In truth, nature destroys man as well as aids him, and the best that can be said is that she— this feminine pronoun, which indicates submissiveness, is an example of the liberal illusion—is indifferent to man. Reason is useful in determining the means to ends that we desire, but it cannot determine a desirable end. Since Sartre identifies himself with modern empirical methodology, which rejects revelation as well as a priori ideas, he regards the view that individuals have inherent rights vested in them by natural law as a form of intellectual confusion.

The ideological function of the natural rights doctrine is described by Sartre in the novel *Nausea.* There he contrasts unfavorably the city fathers of Bouville, who believed in their indefeasible rights, with the rational lucidity of Rocquentin, who finds his very existence to be gratuitous and unjustifiable. Rocquentin enters a gallery devoted to the city fathers of Bouville:

. . . in the large room which I was entering, more than one hundred and fifty portraits were hung on the walls . . . none of those pictured there died a bachelor, none of them died without children or a will, none without the last sacraments. In order, that day as every other day, with God and with the world, these men had slipped softly into death, and once there demanded the eternal life to which they had a right.

For they claimed everything as of right: life, work, wealth, authority, respect, and finally immortality.[6]

Rocquentin notes in his diary:

What these somber canvases offered to my view was man reconsidered by man, with, for their only adornment, the most desirable conquest of man: the bouquet of the Rights of Man and of the Citizen. I admired without reservations the reign of man.[7]

But as for himself, he remarks ". . . I always knew: I did not have the right to exist. I had arrived by accident, I existed like a stone, a plant, a microbe." [8] And his admiration for his "betters" is but irony; as he records his departure from the gallery he writes: "Goodbye beautiful lilies, elegant in your little painted sanctuaries, goodbye lovely lilies, our pride and our reason for existence, goodbye bastards!" [9] Within the context of Sartre's work, those who believe that they possess indefeasible individual rights fall into his category of persons who regard their presence in the world as vital and necessary, when in reality they could very well be dispensed with and should be concerned with justifying their personal behavior and social position.

Since one of the requirements of the existential virtue of authenticity is rational lucidity with respect to the human condition, a belief in the reality of individual rights is not only an error but an existential sin. For the bourgeois of Bouville the concept of "rights" served as an evasion of responsibility for the sufferings of those less well off than himself. This evasion of responsibility is a consequence of the refusal of the bourgeois to recognize that his way of life is the fruit of his own free choice and not justifiable in terms of any natural order of things. The bourgeois in the portraits came from a wealthy and secure class with solid traditions, and lived their lives during the heyday of middle-class society. Never having known the anguish which reveals the gratuity of human projects, they took the privileges of their class for the order of the world. Natural rights doctrine appears in this context as the vehicle for a smug conservatism.

Sartre has shown how the concept of natural rights can serve as a remedy for anguish rather than as a protection against it. The comfortable security of the city fathers of Bouville is not available to the young, the failures, or the status-conscious petty bourgeois. Even the city fathers would find reasons to question the order of nature in a period characterized by economic troubles, war, and the growth in power of political movements which challenge their privileges. The short story "The Childhood of a Leader" describes how under these circumstances the concept of natural rights finds its natural place in extreme rightist or fascist ideology. The story presents the development from early childhood to young adulthood of Lucien, a political rightist and anti-Semite. After a period of uncertainty in which he feels anguish at the realization of his own gratuity he finally discovers himself: "'I HAVE RIGHTS!' Rights! Something of the nature of triangles and circles: they were so wonderful that they didn't exist, . . . rights were beyond existence, like mathematical objects and religious dogmas." [10] This passage insists upon the abstract character of rights, which are conceived as belonging to a person while at the same time having their own independent reality. This independent reality is guaranteed by the natural order of natural rights liberalism. Lucien's belief in rights is more than a rationalization of his self-interest; he actually derives his reality as a person from the "reality" of rights which he possesses. This objective reality of abstract rights is important to him for the same reason as his more or less accidentally acquired reputation as an anti-Semite. It furnishes him with a personal identity and a framework within which to live. He must have these in the form of givens because of his total lack of inner life or personal moral standards.

Sartre has analyzed this personality type at some length in his essay on anti-Semitism. It is substantially the same as the so-called authoritarian personality, or what Hofstadter has described as the "pseudo-conservative." [11] Lucien's character is a classic of this type. He is anti-Semitic, inclined toward violence, incapable of normal emotional relationships, conventional in his standards of judgment, thinks in stereotypes, despises weakness in others, and is a conformist. These characteristics compose a fairly stable character structure with predictable behavior patterns and psychic needs. Lucien accepts the natural rights doctrine as the authoritarian accepts religion:

. . . not because of its objective truth, but on account of its value in realizing goals that might also be achieved by other means. This attitude falls in line with the general tendency toward subordination and renunciation of one's own judgment so characteristic of the mentality of those who follow fascist movements. Acceptance of an ideology is not based upon understanding of or belief in its content but rather upon what immediate use can be made of it, or upon arbitrary decisions. . . .

. . . .

. . . religion is adhered to as a means for maintaining social status and social relationships . . .[12]

Sartre's view of the ideological function of natural rights assumes its status as the more or less official doctrine of middle-class society. Whether it serves the interests of the comfortable bourgeois immersed in daily routine, or buttresses the social position of those who have gone through anguish to bad faith, it involves the identification of the existing social order with the natural order. This identification in Sartre's view is inevitable, since the idea of a natural order is in the first instance derived from the existing social order. The personality of a participant in a particular social order develops within this order. Consequently he finds an order of emotions and points of view within himself, which, when in passive contemplation he ceases to regard the things around him as tools to his own purposes, he finds paralleled in nature. As we find a pattern in our own responses to situations, so we assume a pattern in natural events. Thus, "generations of workers would be able to, . . . scrupulously obey the orders of Lucien without ever using up his right to command . . ."[13] This sort of identification would seem to be illustrated by the important role of property rights in bourgeois conservatism, and by the curious fact that the American pseudoconservative of the McCarthy type noisily praises civil liberties while striving to suppress them.

Sartre's criticism of the natural rights doctrine results from his rejection of the philosophy of nature which underlies it and his judgment that under present social conditions it is more useful to the conservative than to the liberal. In other words, he rejects it in the name of reason and, it would appear, in the name of liberalism, although he calls himself a socialist and would probably prefer to say that early liberalism has become conservatism. His attitude toward the same doctrine in the hands of eighteenth-century writers such as Voltaire is considerably different:

> What the writer of the eighteenth century claims tirelessly in his writings is the right to exercise against history an anti-historic reason and, in a sense, he only illuminates the essential requirements of an abstract literature. He doesn't try to give his readers a clearer class consciousness: on the contrary, the urgent call which he directs toward his middle class public is an invitation to forget humiliations, prejudices and fears; that which he addresses to his aristocratic public is a call to abandon class pride and privileges. As he speaks from the point of view of the universal, he can only have universal readers and what he requires from the freedom of his contemporaries is that they break their historical attachments in order to join him in universality.[14]

Sartre here sees the natural rights doctrine as a critical tool which had negative results insofar as it dissolved the outworn ideology of the ruling class and separated the middle class from their historical resentments. At the same time it was a positive force as it placed on individuals of both classes a moral obligation to transcend their historic situation toward a new social and political order. The claim of writers such as Voltaire to exercise an "anti-historic reason" against historical institutions represented a claim for the free individual intellect against social restraint, and not an attempt to justify an existing social order.

The abstract framework of natural rights was valuable for criticizing particular social institutions, but not adequate to the demands of the new situation once the work of the revolution had been accomplished. The new society brought new forms of oppression, and then a need for new men and new ideas: it is not the function of the writer to build utopias but to reveal to men the nature of their society, and to make them aware of their moral responsibility to change it. "If our desires could be realized, the writer of the twentieth century would occupy . . . a situation analogous to that of the writers of the eighteenth . . ." [15] Sartre does not believe the liberal concern for civil liberties to be outmoded; it constitutes an insight of permanent importance. But freedom of speech, for example, has been in considerable measure achieved, it can be better defended on a different philosophical basis, and it is not enough; the problems of the new oppressed class are economic and social.

In summary, it can be said that Sartre evaluates natural rights liberalism as a political ideology in terms of the validity of its philosophical foundation and in terms of its social function. Insofar as it asserts the ability of individual reason to rise above historical circumstances and evaluate social institutions, he regards it as justified. But when it attempts to assert that certain rights are inherent in a natural moral order, it is unsound. Individual rights are for Sartre a function of a particular social order and not of a universal order of nature. The social function of the concept of natural rights in a society where the particular rights claimed are not recognized in practice differs from its function in a society where these same rights are regarded as secured. In the first case it is progressive; in the second case conservative or reactionary. The philosophical error of early liberalism thus becomes a moral error in the contemporary social environment.

The second important philosophy of the liberal tradition was utilitarianism. Jeremy Bentham, its most influential advocate, shared with Locke a faith in the power of reason to understand society: ". . . the season of *Fiction* is now over . . . To attempt to introduce any *new* one, would be *now* a crime . . ." [16] Bentham rejected natural rights liberalism and instead of relying on a self-evident natural law substituted what he took to be a scientific view of human nature. Individual psychology was to furnish the key to the nature and purpose of social organization.

The utilitarians adopted a view of human nature that had entered philosophy with Hobbes and had been utilized by Locke: the view that the ultimate social reality is the individual and not the community. In addition, Hobbes, Locke, and the utilitarians considered individual self-interest as the prime motivation of individual behavior; in utilitarian thought this psychological egoism was combined with the assumption that individuals seek pleasure and avoid pain. This schematic psychology offered a useful tool for criticism of traditional social institutions and organizations; the role of the government was not considered to be the promotion of individual rights, as in the case of the natural rights doctrine, but rather to take an active part in the creation of a social order suitably adjusted to the requirements of human nature. Individuals would have only the rights given to them by governmental authority. However, since government action necessarily involves the making of rules and the enforcement of penalties for their violation, a new law could be justified only if the balance of individual pleasures over individual pains resulting from the law was clearly positive.

Sartre's disagreements with the utilitarians begin with

their theory of human nature. The view that all individuals by nature pursue their own selfish interests, a view
which has been dear to the hearts of the middle class
and economists, was thought by the utilitarians to mean
that a person naturally seeks the satisfaction of his immediate desires, but that once he has learned or been
taught the possibility of foregoing some present satis-
factions in the interest of greater long-term advantages,
prudence will take over and he can be counted on to
adjust his behavior accordingly. The trouble with this
theory is that it ignores the fact of prerational motivation,
or what Sartre calls the project, as well as the influence
of other persons in the role of subjects on our behavior.
For Sartre as for Freud, reason is more likely to find
that what we want to do anyway is to our advantage,
than to change our desires to suit its calculations. And
what is this self, whose advantage is supposedly the object of our solicitude. Is it the ego? For Sartre the ego
is simply a reflective grasp of my past states, whereas
my desires push me constantly into the future. This
future goal is, on the reflective level, unknown to me.
If an individual was to identify himself radically with
his ego, at the expense of the other dimensions of his
being, he would be in bad faith. This is, of course,
possible, and perhaps in some cultures a prevalent form
of self-deception. The same considerations would apply
if being-for-others was given the status of the self whose
advantage was to be of ultimate concern. Finally, be-
nevolence, love, and masochism are inexplicable in a
realistic way on the basis of the utilitarian theory.

The second assumption of the utilitarians, that individuals pursue pleasure and flee pain, is equally superficial.
To say that people are motivated by desire is not the
same as to say they seek pleasure; people throng physi-

cians' offices with real symptoms due not to illness but
to a desire to suffer. A deliberate pursuit of pleasure is
likely to amount to a desire to forget or avoid some
personal problem. Far from encouraging this attitude,
Sartre urges us to follow desire in the knowledge that
ultimate satisfaction is impossible, to accept the shame
and guilt which comes from being in the world with
others, and to face the anguish which accompanies our
freedom. That Sartre's psychology is superior to that of
the utilitarians should occasion no surprise, since he is
a contemporary and a psychologist. What should be
noted is the degree to which his theory of human reality
undercuts the foundations of utilitarian doctrine.

There was no logical connection between the utilitarian
concept of human nature and their ethics, which asserted
the greatest happiness of the greatest number as the
ultimate value, unless it be a smuggled-in natural law
principle which commanded the Golden Rule. It is
difficult to see how a person solely motivated by his own
interest and the pursuit of pleasure could prefer to suffer
for the good of the greater number. In any case, Sartre
denies that there is any intelligible objective standard of
this sort. Individuals, due to their differing situations
and standards of value, will have differing ideas of what
constitutes the general welfare. To speak of the utility of
something for the greatest happiness of the greatest
number is to justify something which everybody understands by something on which no one can agree. Thus
utility tends to become an end in itself, and functions as
a standard of social value. Now, the acceptance of social
utility as a criterion for value represents for Sartre a
form of bad faith. The socially useful things and techniques that surround the individual imply a view of the
world; that is, everything that is useful is useful *for some*

purpose. Concern with the useful as such tends to mask from the individual the purposes which lie behind a particular utility, and yet leads him to accept these purposes as valid for himself. The immorality of utilitarianism lies in its encouragement of the view that utility lies in *things* rather than in their relation to the individual. ". . . utilitarianism . . . is the *middle term* raised to the all powerful; it has thus in the indissoluble couple of the means and the end chosen to give the first importance to the means. The end is taken for granted, never looked straight in the face, . . ." [17] This view of morality is in sharp contrast to Sartre's version of the existentialist virtue of authenticity. Moral responsibility is for Sartre a prime characteristic of the individual, and this responsibility extends to the social goals which give rise to social utility.

Utilitarian political theory, on the basis of the greatest happiness principle, held that it was the role of government to apportion pains and penalties so that individuals would find their own interests to be identical with the general welfare, a task which has been termed "the artificial identification of interests." This view gives a wide latitude to the legislator in the restriction of individual liberties, and would justify an authoritarian utilitarianism. This course is supported by the fact that utilitarianism tended to confuse moral and legal obligation: Bentham, for example, followed Paley in reducing moral duty to the avoidance of penalties. It is difficult to find room here for the claim of individual liberty against the state which John Stuart Mill was later to defend. The rigid limitations of the natural rights doctrine give way to a doctrine which reduces the sphere of individual freedom to the convenience of the community. The individual has no peculiar contribution to make which gives him a moral claim on the community, and equality replaces liberty as the standard of community organization.

Sartre's position on this issue contrasts markedly with that described above. Due to the diversity of projects, each individual has a unique contribution to make to the social body. This contribution is moral, and the individual bears the responsibility for it. He is not a selfish agent whose welfare lies in the acceptance of discipline, but a moral agent whose autonomy claims respect from the community. There is no ready-made formula that justifies government action. In short, for Sartre, individual political and social freedom is a personal and social good beyond any question of its utility for the promotion of happiness.

The principle of artificial identification of interests, however, not only gives too broad a power to the government, it also unduly limits it. This is a result, in Sartre's view, of a methodological error. A basic similarity between utilitarianism and the earlier natural rights liberalism is, according to Sartre, the point of view on nature and society which determined their approach to human nature and politics.

The middle class, it seems to me, can be defined intellectually by the use which it makes of the spirit of analysis, whose initial postulate is that complexes must necessarily be reducible to an arrangement of simple elements. . . . These in effect—this is the second postulate of analysis—retain unalterably their essential properties, whether they enter into a whole or whether they exist in a free state.[18]

Whether the moral foundation of society is considered to be consent or the greatest happiness principle, society is considered to be an artificial body composed of individual atoms, each one sufficient unto itself.

In the society conceived by the spirit of analysis the individual, solid and indestructible, vehicle of human nature, resides like a pea in a can of peas: he is round, closed in on himself, incapable of communication.[19]

Liberalism, acting from this view of human nature, gives the government a negative role, that of removing obstacles from the path of the individual.

As opposed to this view, Sartre holds that:

. . . a whole, of whatever kind, is different in nature from the sum of its parts. For us, what men have in common is not a nature but a metaphysical condition; and by that we mean the combination of constraints which limit them *a priori,* the necessity to be born and to die, that of being finite and of existing in the world among other men. For the rest, they constitute indestructible totalities whose ideas, moods and acts are secondary and dependent structures, and whose essential character is to be *situated,* and they differ among themselves as their situations differ among themselves.[20]

The dependence of the individual personality on the situation—his milieu, class, nation, and the state of the world—is not merely factual. It is doubled by the moral responsibility of the individual for the world in which he lives.

One doesn't do what one wants but one is responsible for what one is: that is the fact; man who is explainable simultaneously by so many causes is however alone to carry the weight of himself.[21]

The task of the government is thus to act on the total social environment:

Since man is a totality, it is not sufficient, in effect, to give him the right to vote, without touching the other factors which form him: he must deliver himself totally, which is to say that he makes himself other, in acting on his biological constitution as well as on his economic conditioning, on his sexual complexes as well as on the political facts of his situation.[22]

In addition to the inability to envisage a positive role for government, the atomistic view of society results in a neglect of the role played by social classes. This limitation prevents the utilitarian from seeing that groups in society have divergent interests, and results in a blindness to the moral claims as well as the political influence of these groups. Sartre, on the other hand, sees politics in terms of a struggle between groups with conflicting views of the general welfare.

In the light of Sartre's criticisms of natural law liberals, it might seem that he would be more kindly disposed toward their successors. He shares with the utilitarians the general view that all knowledge is derived from experience, and agrees that this methodology invalidates the notion of natural rights. The point of departure for utilitarian social theory is individual psychology, and Sartre also begins with the existing individual defined in psychological terms. Finally, the greatest happiness principle would seem to be more consistent with Sartre's position on the critical function of the intellect than the more rigid natural rights doctrine. It is at once more readily applicable to a wide variety of social institutions and a less convenient refuge for the "salauds" who require a clearly outlined and pre-established moral order. In praising the writers of the eighteenth century Sartre does not distinguish clearly the natural rights thinkers from the utilitarians, so it is fair to assume that he regards the rationalism of the utilitarians in the same light as that of the earlier school of liberalism.

However, it cannot be said that these relative advantages of utilitarian liberalism lead Sartre to treat it more kindly than its predecessor. He describes it as the

justifying myth of the middle class, and takes the view
that if the natural rights doctrine sins by being wrong,
the utilitarian doctrine sins through superficiality. This
superficiality is rooted in the inadequate account which
utilitarianism provides of human nature. Sartre's critique
of the utilitarian concept of human nature is directed
at what he conceives to be its erroneous view of human
motivation, and hence of the nature of morality, and
its neglect of the social nature of man.

In the course of the nineteenth century social events
and intellectual developments combined to force a
thorough-going revision of the doctrinal basis of political
liberalism. In the first place, the industrial revolution
produced large organizations which concentrated vast
amounts of economic power in private hands, and gave
birth to a new underprivileged class which made a working concept of the general welfare vital for political
stability. In the second place, the political triumph of
the liberal philosophy and its identification with French
nationalism at the time of the French Revolution led to
an intellectual reaction against the philosophy. In England Burke, in France Bonald and de Maistre, and in
Germany Hegel advanced the cause of political conservatism with arguments that were later to be integrated
into liberalism itself. Generally speaking, and in spite of
great individual differences, these thinkers stressed the
organic nature of society and the irrational sources of
social cohesion. Their views eventually received powerful support from new developments in science; biology,
psychology, and sociology represented by such thinkers
as Darwin, Marx, and Freud revealed new aspects of
reality—organic development, the causative role of institutions in social change, and the irrational roots of
individual behavior—which cracked the seams of liberal
doctrine.

The most influential early critic of liberalism was undoubtedly Hegel. His influence contributed to the formulation of pragmatism in the United States, idealist liberalism in England and on the continent, Communism and socialism through Marx, Fascist doctrine in the Italy of Mussolini, and of course conservative nationalism in Germany. Aside from the fact that the very success of idealist philosophy, in which Hegel was a dominant figure, made some form of idealist liberalism necessary, there were two aspects of Hegel's thought which made it congenial to liberals in search of a philosophy. The first was Hegel's idealism, which seemed to supply a necessary base for the rational understanding of society. Hegel was not content, like Burke, to devalue the positive social role of individual reason: "one ought to have the firm and invincible faith that there is Reason in history and to believe that the world of intelligence and of self-conscious willing is not abandoned to mere chance . . ." [23] Faith in the intelligibility of historical phenomena had been an essential element in early liberal thought. Both Locke and Bentham had tried to defend the rational purpose of the state against the mythical.

Hegel's faith in the rationality of history took the form of a belief that:

. . . divine Providence is wisdom endowed with infinite power which realizes its own aim, that is, the absolute, rational, final purpose of the world. . . . we must seriously try to recognize the ways of Providence, its means and manifestations in history, and their relation to our universal principle.[24]

Although the historical social development to which Hegel refers as Providence was thought to be accessible to human reason, it was not thought to be subject to the control of individuals. The individual participated for the most part blindly in social processes which gave to his life its moral significance. Thus Hegelian idealism placed a strong emphasis on the important role played by social forces determining individual motivation and moral worth.

This second aspect of Hegel's thought, the view that human nature is fundamentally social, was new to liberalism but answered its need for a reformulation which would adapt it to an industrial society. Hegel had pointed up the deficiencies of the "spirit of analysis" for an understanding of society, and the liberal idealists joined in his rejection of the static and abstract concept of human nature and the mechanistic theory of the state of earlier liberals. The liberal idealists substituted a quasi-organic theory of the state and a developmental view of human nature, and then analyzed the ways in which individual self-realization was dependent on social integration. This enabled them to develop a concept of the general welfare which required positive action by the state to provide the conditions necessary for individual self-development, and a concept of individual freedom which included the requirements of a meaningful social role for the individual and his protection against coercive social forces as well as against unwise legislation.

Individual rights for the idealists were not abstractions but grew out of the ethical relationship of the individual to the community. Rights might vary between societies as would obligations, and both arose from the basic moral right of the individual to fulfill a meaningful social function in the particular society. The idealists circumvented the problem of conflict between individual and social interest, which the utilitarians had been unable to handle satisfactorily, by simply assigning the value of social participation the mediating role: individual desires are justified when consistent with the common good, and the common good is identical with the good of all the members of the community. The role of the government is to make available to all the conditions of moral development, and legal coercion is justified by its necessity for reducing other forms of coercion. The Hegelian view is that individual moral worth is expressed in social integration and service of the general welfare. Like utilitarianism, liberal idealism required no particular set of state policies; its view of human nature and the function of the state lacks the utilitarian congruence with laissez-faire economic doctrine, and gives to the state a positive role in promoting human freedom. Liberal idealism, in spite of its serious modifications of earlier forms of liberalism, carries on the liberal tradition. It presents a rational analysis of political institutions, asserts the primary moral value of the individual, and sets up an ideal standard of the general welfare—a society within which the individual can attain his highest moral development—by which to measure the activities of government.

The idealist revision of liberalism obviously avoids some of Sartre's strictures on earlier liberalism. It repudiates the "spirit of analysis," and sees man in his social context, giving a positive and constructive role to government. It presents a morally superior view of individual personality and human freedom. Nevertheless, Sartre regards idealism as simply one more version of the middle-class myth, which still refuses to come to grips with human and social reality. As Kierkegaard attacked Hegel for attempting to solve man's problems by integrating him into an intellectually constructed Providence and urging him to identify himself with world history, so Sartre rejects the idealist position which sees human welfare as identified with a rationally constructed ideal society.

. . . as the bourgeois is related to natural forces only through the intermediacy of others, as material reality appears to him in the form of manufactured products, as his horizon is a world already humanized which reflects his own image, he restricts himself to gathering from the surface of things the meanings which other men have placed there, . . . he convinced himself that the world was reducible to a system of ideas; . . . Thus he conceives human progress as a vast movement of assimilation: ideas merge and minds grow identical. At the end of this immense digestive process, thought will find its unification and society its total integration.[25]

The typical attitude of the idealist is that the good society, from which social conflicts and social evils will be banished, is a goal which can be attained through the meeting of minds and the progress of science. All men are called upon to cease disputing and to evidence their good will by working in harmony, each in his appointed role in society. What this view fails to take into consideration, according to Sartre, are the insurmountable conflicts in society. These conflicts derive from the fact that society is composed of individuals with different value orientations, so that the ideal society of one would be the hell of the other. No matter how many facts are learned about man and society, this pluralism will remain, as the conflict of liberties is not amenable to reason.

Because it contains this basic fallacy, idealist doctrine deceives the dissatisfied into acceptance of the status quo by giving them the hope that, through the progress of knowledge, society will right itself. Sartre does not hesitate to term this trait of idealism disgusting, since it turns men away from authentic existence and perpetuates bad faith. The authentic individual will accept his situation as it is in order to change it in accordance with his own values and by his own efforts. Idealism deceives him by conferring value upon an already existing state of affairs. Conservative idealists, such as Hegel, did this explicitly; liberal idealists tended to distinguish between the ideal society and any actual society, but through their emphasis on the value of social integration and their lack of a realistic view of the requirements of social reform, moved in the same direction.

The deficiencies in the idealist ideology are traceable to their theory of human nature, which leads them to envisage individual moral development in terms of social conformism. Like natural law or social utility as criteria of value, social integration represents ultimately a refuge for bad faith. Encouraging individuals to find their values in the social order is equivalent to hiding from them the fact that their values must arise from their own free choice of themselves in relation to the social order. Sartre's conception of human freedom differs dramatically from that of the idealists. He is at pains to separate the individual from his social role:

. . . from within, the waiter in the café can not be immediately a café waiter in the sense that this inkwell *is* an inkwell, . . . It is by no means that he can not form reflective judgements or concepts concerning his condition. He knows well what it "means:" the obligation of getting up at five o'clock, of sweeping the floor of the shop . . . the right to the tips, the right to belong to a union, etc. . . . It is a matter of abstract possibilities, of rights and duties conferred on a "person possessing rights." . . . But if I represent myself as him, I am not he: I am separated from him as the object from the subject, separated by *nothing,* but this nothing isolates me from him. I can not be he, I can only play *at being* him.[26]

The nothingness which separates the individual from his social role is free human consciousness, which by its free choice of goals surpasses the factual toward the ideal and brings value into the world. The individual is not exhausted by his social role but on the contrary, defines himself insofar as he projects going beyond his situation. Thus Sartre sees a moral challenge not in the effort to integrate into society but in the inevitable separation between the individual and his social role. Being a table waiter, professor, or judge is indeed for Sartre an important aspect of individuality. The actions which a person performs depend upon his social role, and these actions are basic in the constitution of his being-for-others. The modification of one's being-for-others is essential to individual self-realization. However, the moral significance of actions performed is not determined by their social function, but rather by the goals of the individual project. Since these goals are in principle unobtainable, there is never a simple coincidence between them and the functions performed; being-for-others is for the individual a form of degradation. At the same time the individual is responsible for his being-for-others, for his social role, and indeed for the social structure itself. The only remedy, and a partial one at that, for the internal tension which this situation entails is commitment to a more or less clearly formulated program of social reform. Sartre's view of the relation between the individual and society couples an insistence on human nature as a social product with an equally strong emphasis on individual moral creativity.

Sartre does not insist on the individual's lack of moral identity with his social role in order to encourage the cultivation by the individual of essentially private virtues. The nothingness secreted by man in the face of the social order projects him beyond it; but his goals are defined in terms of the social order and realized through it. In other words, the value of integration is replaced by that of engagement, not retirement. Democratic government like any other institutional arrangement receives its moral justification and its essential character from the goals around which it is organized. Since moral goals are the product of free individuals, any doctrine which finds goals immanent in institutional structures is unsound and dangerous to individual moral responsibility. Pragmatism, which advocates social integration and looks to science for the solution of moral problems, and positivism, which regards value structures as merely social facts, would undoubtedly seem to Sartre to present this danger. The ideology of the "organization man," which would appear to have roots in the social theory of pragmatism, represents an extreme example of the tendencies in later liberalism which Sartre is attacking.

The three types of liberalism which have been described here are still influential as ideologies, although as philosophies they are relatively dead and buried. It cannot be said that natural rights liberalism is completely dead, because it is being revived by some prominent American social scientists. It is not possible to report Sartre's views on pragmatism and positivism as social theories, now dominant in the United States, because he has not presented his views on the subject. Anyone familiar with these philosophies, however, can discern the more important differences between them and Sartrean existentialism. It is understandable that Sartre should address himself to the French tradition of liberalism, because it is his tradition, that is, in Sartre's terminology, because it is his situation. The English-speaking reader should bear in mind that the term liberalism is used differently in the Anglo-Saxon world, where it tends to apply to anyone favoring social reform, than in France,

where it is identified with the specific social views characteristic of the middle class.

Sartre finds all forms of liberalism to be, as ideological
phenomena, an outgrowth of the historic situation of the
middle class. Early liberalism is presented as a progressive force prior to the French Revolution in France, and
by analogy, elsewhere during the period when the middle
class was making its conquest of power. During the
period of middle-class dominance liberalism ceased to be
progressive and endured as the justifying myth of a
dominant class. In all three of its forms it represents the
spirit of seriousness, or an attempt to avoid recognition
of the subjective source of values by locating them in
the objective—the law of nature, the happiness principle,
the good society. All three forms of liberalism are accused of allowing no room for the development of the
new oppressed class to political and social consciousness,
either by denying its existence as a class or by requiring
it to conform to a pre-established social harmony ad-
vantageous to the dominant class. Sartre is unwilling to
admit that liberalism has made or can make the transition
from a class to a national ideology. He is not inclined to
put forward his own philosophy as a reformulation of
liberalism. This in spite of the fact that many times his
criticisms seem to aim at showing that early liberalism
was not liberal enough. He has mentioned private property, democracy, progress, and freedom of thought as the
basic themes of liberalism, and the final chapter will
show that these are all important themes in his own
political theory. He favors what is usually referred to
as economic democracy, and considers it a step which
must inevitably lead beyond liberalism.

There has been much criticism of Sartre as a writer
and as a philosopher by people who would probably call

themselves liberals. However, no representative of liberalism has dealt with his arguments in significant detail as have, for example, the Catholics and the Marxists. This is certainly in part because liberals would tend to accept many of his criticisms of past forms of liberal ideology, and in part because the liberals themselves are now in search of a philosophy. In addition, Sartre's position as a onetime "fellow traveler" of the Communists has discouraged many possible sympathizers. Finally, the existentialist movement as a whole has not found a warm reception in liberal circles because of what are conceived to be its pessimistic and irrational features. If and when liberals examine Sartre's arguments with a sympathetic eye, as many religious thinkers have done, perhaps they will try to meet some of his arguments.

The Modern Proteus

CHAPTER VIII

According to mythology, Proteus was a god of the sea who, having received from Neptune the gift of prophecy, escaped from those eager to know his secrets by changing at will into a variety of forms. Sartre finds the Communist view of man in the world to be as elusive as the ancient Proteus. Instead of finding the Marxism professed by the Communists a logically coherent system, he considers it a bundle of contradictory positions. Before we consider the nature of the contradictions which Sartre distinguishes in the views of the Marxists, it should be noted that Sartre does not necessarily maintain that the responsibility for them lies with Karl Marx. Marx has been interpreted in many different ways, and Sartre himself has considered writing a book on Marx, supposedly to correct what he regards as the misinterpretations of others. The Marxism which Sartre criticizes is that of the Communist Party, or what he has described as "Stalinist neo-Marxism."

Marxist materialism appears first of all as a naturalism; it rejects supernatural causes, and denies the existence of God. This atheism is the result of a definite and a priori position taken with respect to a problem which goes far beyond the testimony of our experience. Such a categorical denial of the existence of God seems to Sartre philosophically unjustifiable, precisely because experience can offer no final answer to the question of the existence of God. It is true that Sartre also declares himself to be an atheist. He admits, however, that in doing so he is going beyond the certainty of experience to the realm of the hypothetical and probable. The existence or nonexistence of God is a metaphysical question, and he regards metaphysics as an imaginative enterprise incapable of yielding certainty. Sartre's ontology differs from a metaphysics in that it is a description of facts, and thus is subject to criteria of truth or falsity. His atheism results from a respect for the claims of rationality, plus a basic reluctance to assume more than is justified by the clear testimony of experience; the Marxists, on the other hand, base their atheism on faith as part of the same psychological movement in which they assert the truth of their materialism.

Marxist materialism is then a metaphysical doctrine which reduces mind to matter and eliminates subjectivity by reducing the world, including man, to a system of objects interconnected by universal relations. The Marxists contend that this is the scientific view of the world, and that the success of science establishes its validity. Sartre agrees that the method of science is rational analysis of an externally existing world of objects. He contends that the Marxists go too far, however, when they make the transition from the scientific method to the structure of the universe. Such a position is in fact inconsistent with its supposed scientific basis. The contention that the universe is as science describes it is unscientific, since scientific theories must be tentative and hypothetical in nature. Newton's universe as a dogma could bar the way to other useful scientific hypotheses as effectively as any religious dogmatism. Also, the materi-

alist view of man as an object is illegitimately trans-
formed into a concept of man as the objective observer
of the world. In fact, if man is an object, all possibility
of a rational understanding of the world disappears:

. . . if psychic facts are the effect of biological causes and
biological facts, in turn, of the physical state of the world, I
can see that human consciousness can express the world in
the way that an effect expresses its cause, but not in the way
that a thought expresses its object. A captive reason, governed
from the outside, maneuvered by blind chains of cause and
effect, how would this still be reason? [1]

The dogmatic faith in reason which enables Marxism to
claim certain knowledge of a metaphysical nature about
the world is thus incompatible with the type of world
which it claims to discover. At the same time, the scientific method is converted into a tool for gaining exact
knowledge of the nature of the material world, a pro-
cedure which undermines science itself.

Sartre reaches this conclusion without distinguishing
between "naive" materialism and dialectical materialism
because he considers the Hegelian dialectic incompatible
with materialism. Marx turned the Hegelian dialectic up-
side down, and for the absolute idea substituted matter.
Sartre sees merit in the Hegelian version of the dialectic,
insofar as it embodies a description of the conditions
under which human thought takes place; for example, an
idea in my mind is not an isolated or accidental occurrence but can be explained only in terms of my total
perspective. But the Hegelian dialectic depends for its
force as a concept on the nature of mind and the process
of idea formation. Where it is applied to matter it loses
its plausibility. Science is not dialectic but analytic, and
its systems are mechanical constructs rather than dialectical syntheses. Thus constituted it has been successful,

and the Marxists themselves usually revert to mechanical relationships in their scientific analysis while affirming, in the abstract, dialectical progression. Even on the abstract level, however, plausibility can be maintained only by an inconsistent use of the term "matter," which functions sometimes in the scientific sense as the most general and therefore the simplest abstraction, at other times as a complex and all-inclusive concrete whole. This latter usage resembles the Idea of Hegel, whose perfection was the source and end of the dialectical process. As applied to matter, however, this complexity and universality is already present at the beginning of the dialectic, and cannot serve as its motor.

Sartre distinguishes between "natural history" and the history of human beings and collectivities; only human beings have a history in the sense of a past recovered from the point of view of the present. If the dialectic was to be considered as a method of historical understanding, its value would depend on the fact that history is a human enterprise and not on any supposed characteristics of matter as universal reality. Only idealism, which defines all reality as thought, can consistently identify the dialectical laws of reason with natural processes. Finally, the use by man of the dialectical method as a means of understanding the nonhuman sets up a subject-object relationship that did not exist in Hegel, for whom mind and reality are the same. Consequently, dialectical progression in nature or history can at best only be considered probable, a hypothesis to be verified according to the laws of evidence. Since the sciences of nature proceed from a spirit contrary to that of the dialectic, and since the science of history can justify no such definitive conclusion, the dialectic cannot be considered inherent in the structure of the universe.

Marxist dialectical materialism is a variety of epistemological realism, which asserts that the world exists in-
dependently of the perceiver. It can be distinguished
from idealism, or the view that the world is identical
with the contents of mind or consciousness. Sartre rejects
both views, and occupies a middle ground. Both the subject and the object exist, and neither by itself constitutes
all of reality. Using the terms of the Hegelian triad, we
might say that being is the thesis, consciousness the
antithesis, and the individual in his environment, man-in-
the-world, the synthesis. Sartre objects to materialism
because it suppresses the subject and therefore cannot
account for meaning and purpose, science and morality,
which make the world human.

Apart from this initial error, Sartre sees Marxist philosophy as a conglomerate of disparate elements, rather
than as a coherent philosophical position. Insofar as the
Marxists profess to confine themselves to the methods of
science they should join the positivists in eschewing
metaphysical speculation. Instead of this they assert the
material nature of reality, denying the existence of God
and, at the same time, of free human subjectivity. Finally
they profess, in the form of the dialectic, a dogmatic
rationalism which contradicts both of the above. Such
a position is itself irrational and inconsistent with the
facts of experience to the point where it can only be
accepted on faith. What is the explanation of this faith?
Sartre answers this question by analysis of the subjective
and objective aspects of the Marxist-in-situation.

The contention that the elements of Marxism are self-
contradictory, and the refusal to grant it the status of a
philosophy, raise the question of how to account for the
origin and relative success of the Marxist myth. The
answer must be sought in terms of the nature of human

reality, as in the case of Catholicism, but also in social institutions and particularly the class structure, as in the case of liberalism. Marxism appears finally as the myth suitable to the revolutionary attitude, whose *raison d'être* is not to be found in a scientific attempt to understand society but rather in a search for a justifying belief: "Get down on your knees and you will believe, says Pascal. The enterprise of the materialist is very similar."[2]

The existence of Marxism as a social myth depends in the first place upon the existence of a revolutionary situation. One basic condition of such a situation is the oppression of one class by another. Not all oppressed groups and classes are in a revolutionary situation, however. Their position must be such that their being oppressed is a condition of the social structure.

. . . it is not given to just anybody to become a revolutionary. . . . What the American Negroes and the middle-class Jews desire is an equality of rights . . . they wish simply to be granted the privileges of their oppressors, that is to say that basically they seek a more complete integration.[3]

Segregation of the Negro is inconsistent both with American ideals and with economic progress under our present social system, so the improvement of the Negro's situation requires no basic change in that system. For a revolutionary situation to exist, there must be an oppressive society which includes a privileged class whose privileges are such that they cannot be extended to society as a whole, with the result that equality can be achieved only by the destruction of the privileged class. The second basic condition of a revolutionary situation is that the oppressed class be composed of laborers. This is necessary because it is in the course of his work that an individual discovers his ability to order things to his own ends, and so can conceive of the project of reordering society. Such a reaction to an objective situation on the part of an individual worker, however, cannot be explained in terms of the situation alone. "The two facts of being a worker and of being oppressed suffice to define the situation of the revolutionary but not the revolutionary himself." [4]

An explanation of Marxism as the revolutionary myth must rest primarily on a description of the way in which the worker reacts to his situation. This is because no state of fact is capable of producing in an individual or a group a will to revolution.

> In so far as man is immersed in the historical situation, he does not even succeed in conceiving of the failures and lacks in a political organization or determined economy; this is not, as is stupidly said, because he "is accustomed to it," but because he apprehends it in its plenitude of being and because he can not even imagine that he can exist in it otherwise. . . . it is after he has formed the project of changing the situation that it will appear intolerable to him. . . . he must posit an ideal state of affairs . . .[5]

If the situation itself is not capable of determining any particular reaction on the part of the worker, attention must be directed to the subjective movement within the worker which makes him a revolutionary.

According to Sartre's theory of human reality, all behavior is motivated by the individual project. The meaning of an individual's behavior is determined by the future which he is striving to realize. This is the phenomenon of transcendence; the individual is not a ready-made personality, but a process directed toward the realization of certain goals. This process is synonymous with the reality of human consciousness. It is important to remember that Sartre uses the term "nothingness" to describe human consciousness. Since consciousness is "nothingness," it does not have inherent goals, but must freely choose them. Another important consequence of "nothingness" is that the contents of consciousness, including the content of its goals, are received from the world. Thoughts are in a language, and thinking is in terms of the facts of experience: social position, education, the persons with whom one associates, generally accepted social values, are the stuff of which personality is made. "Human nature" is social in origin. What the individual contributes is his own vision of a "better" world. He may or may not be aware of it on the reflective level, but his most profound desire is to make the world in which he lives—and his society—really *his*, by reconstructing it in accordance with his goals. The goals themselves, while freely chosen by the individual, are framed in terms of the world and envisage an ideal state of the world with the subject as an integral part of it.

Turning from human reality in general to the worker-in-situation, the importance of the situation in the making of a revolutionary is evident: only if progress toward the individual's goals is not possible in a given state of society without radical changes in the social structure will he become a revolutionary. It would thus be wrong to sum up Sartre's theory as "every man a revolutionary." In a free society, reform would be the goal rather than revolution. Political and social freedom exists when individuals are able to commit themselves to a course of action and to progress toward the realization of their goals. It is, then, the denial of freedom which makes an individual into a revolutionary.

Given the existence of a revolutionary social class, or more accurately, a class of revolutionary individuals, a revolutionary doctrine is both a precondition and an outgrowth of the development of a revolutionary movement.

The prerational evaluation of his situation as undesirable in terms of the projected ideal relationship to a reconstructed society tends to be rationalized and to receive an explicit formulation. The actual attempt to bring about changes in the social system requires immediately at least a minimum of deliberate planning of strategy, and over a period of time will tend to take the form of a full-blown doctrine. In short, the decision to revolt carries with it a point of view toward society as that which is to be revolted against. But there is no question here of the proletarian, as a member of a disinherited class with no interests to defend, being able to take an "objective" view of society. Understanding, according to Sartre, is only possible within the context of the individual's project. Our situation, or society as it appears to us:

. . . can not be subjective, for it is neither the sum nor the unity of the *impressions* which things make on us. It is *the things themselves* and myself among things; . . .
But neither can the situation be *objective* in the sense that it would be a pure given which the subject would establish without being in any way engaged in the system thus constituted. . . . The situation is the subject illuminating things by his very surpassing, if you like; it is things referring to the subject his own image.[6]

The point of view which the proletarian takes of history might be termed ideological, as it is a function of his personal desires and situation, and at the same time a social doctrine or philosophy of life.

While this ideology is the product of an individual subjectivity, it will tend to merge into a class doctrine insofar as the members of that class share the same situation. This would be particularly true of a revolutionary class, since the requirements of revolutionary action are collective in nature and the success of this action would be a prerequisite to any further pursuit of individual goals. The individuality of points of view would inevitably reassert itself, however, after the goal of revolution had been achieved, although new groups might form on the basis of the new situations. The new groups might not require a revolutionary ideology, but there would continue to be differences on matters of policy: new problems would bring with them new ideas and social theories.

If Sartre follows the Marxists in tracing liberalism to roots in the social position of the bourgeoisie, he uses the same type of analysis to explain Marxism as a proletarian ideology. It should be noted that he considers his own political theory to be true, universal, and suitable for both bourgeois and proletarian. His theory, however, does not envisage any final solution to the problem of conflicting individual and group concepts of the general welfare, but rather a continual effort to remove the most glaring injustices, and thus assumes the persistence of ideological divisions within society. He compares his view to Marx's "beyond Communism" and Trotsky's "permanent revolution."

The materialist metaphysics of Marxism is considered by Sartre to be a product of the exigencies of a revolutionary movement. Moreover, it is the only myth suitable to the requirements of the revolutionary. One of the first requirements of the revolutionary is to free himself from the social values which buttress the position of the privileged class and stand in the way of revolutionary action.

. . . the essential fear of man, above all if he is suffering, is not so much death or the existence of a strict God, but simply that the state of things from which he suffers has been produced and is maintained for transcendent and unknown ends: any effort to change it would then be guilty and vain; a subtle discouragement would penetrate him, affecting even his judgments, and would prevent him from desiring and even from conceiving an improvement.[7]

Materialism removes the sting from established social norms by abolishing their supernatural sanctions, merging man into nature, and explaining all of nature in terms of a rigid causal chain at whose origin is an original contingency. The chance origin of the universe and the determined character of its subsequent development reduce social phenomena, including values, to morally neutral chains of cause and effect. The Greek materialist Epicurus did not dare to abolish the gods, but rendered them harmless by reducing them to products of the movement of atoms.

Another aspect of the revolutionary attitude which leads to the myth of materialism is what Sartre terms, after Comte, the explanation of the higher by the lower. The revolutionary finds himself in a society where the material and spiritual aspects of life have been separated; the working class, because of its identification with those aspects of society devoted to the provision of the basic necessities of life and the relative poverty of its members, is primarily aware of the material, while the upper class with its wealth and leisure produces ideology, culture, and values. This class culture has little attraction for the revolutionary, since it offers him the image of his own oppression. He gives priority to an explanation of society—in terms of its economic, technical, and biological aspects—which reflects and validates his own role in society. Materialism is simply the extension from society to the universe as a whole of this explanation of the higher by the lower. It appears as synonymous with the conviction of the revolutionary that the so-called higher activities of man are actually dependent on and subsidiary to the provision of the material necessities of life.

Finally, the revolutionary learns through experience the reality of nonsubjective factors and their impact on human life. As a worker he must contend with an objective order of nature which can be controlled only by obedience to its laws. As a member of an oppressed class, he must live the harsher side of the social order. "Death, unemployment, the repression of a strike, . . . are everyday realities which are experienced with horror. . . . they retain above all a stubborn and irrational reality." [8] The problem of action thus becomes one of subduing an intransigent world, and the nature of action a constant struggle requiring all human resources, rather than the manipulation of ideas aimed at explaining away a stubborn environment. Materialism, which affirms the priority of the object over the subject, appears as a philosophic exaggeration of revolutionary realism.

This revolutionary realism differs from conservative realism in that it is accompanied by reformism, or the project of achieving a better society in the future. Hobbesian realism is also materialistic, but aimed at the maintenance of the existing social order. Since the revolutionary wants to change society, he projects the course of history as progress. Sartre distinguishes between the rebel and the revolutionary: for the rebel, the act of rebellion is an end in itself, and since this rebellion must be against something, he guards a secret respect for and dependence upon established values; a revolutionary is someone who wants to change the world by transcending it in the direction of a new world order based on a new set of values. The Marxist dialectic fulfills the requirement of the revolutionary in the form of a myth, by vesting in objective historical factors an inherent drive toward a better future. Thus reformism,

far from conflicting with materialism, utilizes it as a way
of insisting on the cruel realities of the existing social
order.

It should be noted here that materialism is possible as
a revolutionary doctrine because of a basic assumption
which Sartre does not share; namely, the beneficence of
the natural order. This is evident above all in the important role which the dialectic holds in the Marxist
system; it is basically a version of natural law which
retains its descriptive and normative functions. Sartre's
view of nature has already been discussed; it is present
at the heart of his philosophy, in the distinction which
he makes between being-in-itself and being-for-itself.
Being-in-itself, which corresponds to nature, has the
being of objective fact, whereas being-for-itself, or human
consciousness, is the source of all values. Marxist dialectical materialism betrays a nonreflective optimism about
the relations between man and the natural order which
may be a requirement of the revolutionary attitude.
Sartre, who holds out his philosophy as a superior alternative to Marxism, nowhere explicitly traces materialism
to this origin. Nevertheless, this point is implicit in all
his criticisms of Marxism as a social doctrine.

Marxist materialism, then, has its roots in the revolutionary attitude. But it is the doctrine of the revolutionary in bad faith. When Marxists are cornered in a
philosophical discussion, says Sartre, they are likely to
declare that materialism is a point of view, or a way of
life. Sartre agrees: "They would not be so far wrong,
and I would consider it willingly, for my part, one of
the forms of the serious mentality and of the flight before
one's self." [9] Here again, as in the case of Catholicism
and the various forms of liberalism, we have a political

ideology which reflects the desire of men to fly from themselves, to escape from their freedom.

Bad faith is possible because of the ambiguity of human reality; at one and the same time man is and is not his past, his transcendence, his being-for-others. Bad faith consists in affirming one aspect of human reality at the expense of the others. The Marxist form of bad faith involves a denial of transcendence:

The serious attitude involves starting from the world and attributing more reality to the world than to oneself; at the very least the serious man confers reality on himself to the degree to which he belongs to the world. It is not by chance that materialism is serious; . . . This is because revolutionaries are serious. They come to know themselves first in terms of the world which oppresses them, and they wish to change this world.[10]

Marxists are immersed in history. They identify themselves with the object which they appear to be to their oppressors, which is their being-for-others, and by their materialist faith deny their own subjectivity. The judgment of the employer, for whom the worker is a commodity on the labor market, becomes the judgment of the worker on himself. As an object he becomes an integral part of the materialist world of objects, a man-thing. The doctrine of materialism does for the worker what God did for Daniel and natural rights for Lucien:

. . . the desire of each one of us is to exist *with his entire consciousness* in the mode of being a thing. To be entirely consciousness and at the same time entirely stone. To this dream, materialism is in principle satisfactory, since it says to man that he is only a mechanism. Thus I have the somber pleasure of *feeling* myself think and of knowing myself a material system.[11]

A materialist universe thus serves the same purpose as a God-centered universe, that of relieving the individual of responsibility for himself and his situation.

The revolutionary in bad faith is in the paradoxical position of looking forward to a better world while denying his own transcendence, which alone could furnish him with a standard for a better world. Marxism enables him to live this paradox by putting the responsibility for moral progress upon history; the evil present prepares a flawless future. In spite of the fact that they belong to a revolutionary party, the Marxists deny their creative role in history, and distrust values. And by reducing men to the status of objects in the world, the pawns of their environment, they destroy individual responsibility. These men who look to history for security, justification, and relief from responsibility are in bad faith. As in his criticism of the Catholics, Sartre is apparently not convinced that all Marxists are in bad faith, but rather that both the doctrine and the Party encourage it.

The comparison between two Communists who figure in Sartre's literary works, Brunet in *The Roads to Freedom* and Hoederer in *Dirty Hands,* illustrates Sartre's understanding of the Marxist in bad faith. When Brunet's friend challenges the action of the Soviet Union in signing a nonaggression pact with Nazi Germany, Brunet answers:

. . . I am not going to argue with you about that: I am a man of action and I have never wasted my time engaging in speculation about high policy: . . . I trust the Central Committee and the U.S.S.R.; . . . it is not impossible that the members of the Politbureau have all gone crazy. But, in the same way, it is no more impossible that the roof of this shack should fall on your head; however, you don't spend your life staring at the ceiling. . . . you know very well that there are natural laws and that buildings remain standing when they are built according to these laws. . . . I know that there are historical laws and that, in virtue of these laws, the workers' state and the European proletariat have identical interests. Moreover, I don't think about it often, no more than you think about the foundations of your house . . .[12]

Brunet equates moral principles with the laws of physics, and sees no difference between constructing the good society and building a bridge. He relies on the intelligence and virtue of the Party leaders implicitly and without reflecting. Since his orders are a priori good, he feels no personal responsibility for the actions of the Party to which he gives his support. He has abandoned any personal attempt to understand himself and the world, and the wisdom of his actions, and those of his Party, are as certain as the sunrise in the morning. He is a militant, but no longer a man.

The statements of Hoederer, who is also a militant and devoted to the cause of the revolution, reflect an altogether different sense of his relation to history:

If you do not want to run risks [of being wrong] you should not engage in politics.

A party is never more than a means.

Myself, I have dirty hands. . . . Do you imagine that one can govern innocently?

We others, we find it less easy to shoot at a man for reasons of principle because it is we who make ideas and we know what goes into them: we are never altogether sure of being right.[13]

For Sartre, Hoederer represents the authentic man. As opposed to Brunet, he does not believe that action in the name of or according to the principles of the Party is necessarily efficacious or justified. The responsibility for the rightness or wrongness of his actions which accordingly rests on his shoulders is accepted as the price of achievement. He is conscious that the principles of the Party in the name of which he acts are, in the most important sense, a personal wager, and when he must advance them at the expense of others he acts in anguish. Nevertheless, he continues to lead the fight for the cause in which he believes.

In summary, Marxist metaphysical materialism, belief in the determinism of the dialectic, and faith in science are considered by Sartre to be the doctrinal embodiment of bad faith, since they function as avenues of escape from personal moral responsibility. The Marxist is a revolutionary in bad faith, who seeks relief from his difficult circumstances and a meaning in life by submerging his identity in a *deus ex machina,* the Communist movement. Composed of such men, the Communist Party can be unscrupulous about the means of obtaining power and, when successful, is insensitive to the moral justifications which the exercise of power requires. From a revolutionary party it evolves into a conservative government. "Marx proposed the original dogma of the serious when he asserted the priority of object over subject." [14]

Sartre and the Marxist Man

CHAPTER IX

In spite of Sartre's condemnation of Marxist ideology
there are important resemblances, as well as differences,
between his social doctrine and that of the Communists.
Sartre asserts that his is the natural philosophy of the
revolutionary, although it is also suitable to all men, and
there is no question that it is a doctrine of social reform.
Consequently, it seems logical to expect certain similarities with Marxism, which is, at least in the hands of
Marx, strongly oriented toward conscious change. In
order to see where Sartre agrees with Marx and where
he disagrees, it will prove profitable to compare the
Sartrean and Marxist doctrines with respect to their concepts of history, social class, and alienation.

Marxism shares with liberalism the basic assumption
that reason is adequate to the understanding of historical
reality which is thus made subject to conscious human
direction. The Marxists, however, follow Marx, Hegel,
and liberal idealism in rejecting the "spirit of analysis"
which was characteristic of early liberalism, and which
resulted in considering society as a collection of individuals, each constituting an instance of a universal human
nature. The method which the Marxists substitute for the
analytical is the dialectical: society is conceived as a
functioning whole which develops through time and

whose parts are characterized by reciprocal interaction. If this was all that the Marxists understood by the dialectic, it could be considered an early approximation to the functional theory of society which has been developed by an American sociologist, Talcott Parsons. The functional theory considers society as a "going concern," and attempts to find functional relationships between different social phenomena; i.e., a certain moral theory might be favored or retarded in its expansion by social conditions resulting from the economic structure of society. This theory would not exclude but complement studies aimed at elucidating mechanical or cause-effect relationships, such as the relationship between a social identification of physical aggressiveness with masculinity and crimes of violence.

However, the dialectic means more to Marxists than is suggested by an explanation in terms of the functional theory of society. Instead of being a working hypothesis for historical studies, it becomes the inner principle of all social activity. In other words, it is not thought of as a conceptual tool, subjective in origin, but as a characteristic of objective historical reality. As such it becomes a standard of validity for human thought, or, in Marxist terminology, a logic. The causative factor by which Marxists account for historical development is a consequence of Marxist materialism, which posits man's activities in providing for the material necessities of life as basic. The economic organization of society results in a system of social classes, whose conflict is the motor of social change. Other aspects of social life belong to the superstructure, and cannot exercise an ultimately determining influence. The predominant role of the economic activities of man enables prediction of historical development through analysis of economic changes and their social effects.

Sartre is willing to say with the Marxists that "each age develops according to dialectical laws," [1] but the meaning which he gives to the term dialectic differs from the Marxist usage. The nature of this difference in meaning is indicated by his statement that:

. . . every theory, be it scientific or philosophic, is probable. The proof is that scientific and historical theses vary, and that they are offered in the form of hypotheses.[2]

Sartre is willing to accept the dialectic, with its implications of change, the social system as a functioning whole, and interaction between the various aspects of social life, but only as a theoretical construct subjective in origin. In short, Sartre accepts the dialectic in the same way that Talcott Parsons accepts the functional theory of society, as a tool for understanding the nature and development of social systems. In this context economic determinism becomes simply one aspect of the social whole whose influence on other aspects of society is a matter for empirical investigation. Historical laws are only probable and subject to disproof by more adequate hypotheses.

Within the context of Sartre's existentialist theory of history, the dialectic serves as a method for investigating the "situation" of a period, or "the ensemble of material and even psychoanalytical conditions which, in a given age, give a specific character to an ensemble." [3] In addition to an examination of the situation, understanding of a historical period depends on proper consideration of the nature of human reality. Sartre considers that love, for example, is not a product of social factors, but a permanent structure of human reality which can be masked, idealized, or otherwise channeled by the situation of the period. Since the human condition is a constant through all historical periods and is not affected by the relativity characteristic of the situation, it offers an avenue of approach toward the understanding of a period in history. The historian can identify himself with the "project" of a society, and then examine the situation in the light of that project, thus re-creating the life of a past society as it seemed to those who lived in it. Sartre has not attempted this type of study of a historical period, but has used substantially the same method in his biography of Jean Genet. To make the transition from biography to history all that is necessary is to substitute the ideology of a group for the individual project.

In summary, Sartre accepts much of Marxist historiography but rejects the Marxist philosophy of history. His approach to a culture stresses its ideology as the synthesis of the objective and subjective factors in historical reality, whereas the Marxists stress the mode of production and explain subjective factors in terms of it. The absolute in history is for Sartre the human condition, while for the Marxist the absolute is the economic base in its evolutionary forms. Sartre preserves what might be termed the spiritual orientation of Hegel but substitutes the existing individual for the Idea, while the Marxists preserve the objective development characteristic of the Hegelian Idea but abandon the spiritual for a material orientation. Objective development, or changes in social institutions which result from the nature of these institutions themselves and are independent of the purposes of a particular generation, is not excluded from Sartre's thought but is relegated to the realm of the probable.

A comparison between the Marxist concept of social class and that of Sartre presents the same picture of some obvious areas of agreement together with some important disagreements. The concept of social class in Marxism functions as a surrogate for the liberal concept of human nature. The social whole is broken down into classes which are essentially antagonistic, and social change, made inevitable by changes in the mode of production, is a result of their conflicts. Classes are economic in origin, produced by the social division of labor. While not assuming that all individual behavior is explicable by motivations toward the realization of economic interests, Marx felt that the meaning of the behavior of members of a class in the aggregate would be the preservation or realization of the economic interests of the class. His position on this point resembles that of contemporary sociologists in making generalizations about the predictability of group behavior, generalizations whose validity is considered to be independent of individual differences in expressed motives for behavior, and the problem of freedom of the will. Marx's view as to the predictability of class behavior within the area of class economic interests could thus be regarded as scientific, but only as long as it stays within the limits of empirically established generalizations and does not attempt to predict individual behavior.

There is a danger here, however, of sliding into the unscientific position that all individual members of a particular social class are, consciously or unconsciously, motivated by the advancement of the economic interests of that class, and further, that the very existence of a class will inevitably give rise to group behavior which will be equivalent to the intelligent pursuit of class economic interests. Neither one of these propositions could

very well be proved, and if accepted would result in a
rigid form of economic determinism. The tendency of
Marxists to adopt a deterministic view is increased by
other aspects of Marx's social doctrine. In the first place,
he denies that there is any such thing as a universal
human nature, which might supply a common ground
between members of classes. The individual consciousness
is social in origin, and in a class society this means that
it is a class consciousness. Instead of human nature, there
is bourgeois nature and proletarian nature. In the second
place, Marx's concept of ideology asserts that supposedly
universal moral principles are irrational in origin, a
simple expression of class interests. Finally, the Marxist
concept of the classless society, in which class interests
and conflicts have disappeared, envisages the end of
ideology and a universality of human nature; true
science and morality are the products of changes in the
social structure. As a result of these various features of
Marxism, all of which de-emphasize the role of individual subjectivity, we are left with the picture of classes
which inevitably pursue their economic interests, and
whose members, being creatures of their class, have this
pursuit as their real goal in life, regardless of their subjective intentions; in other words, human nature is
equated with class membership. Irrationality and conflict
disappear only with the disappearance of classes.

Sartre agrees with Marx that social classes exist, that
at least some of them are the product of the economic
system, that human nature is related to class membership,
and that ideology is an outgrowth of the class structure.
Nevertheless, the differences between Sartre's concept of
social class and the Marxist concept are profound. Sartre
is in fact closer to the liberals than to Marx because
he sees society as broken down into individuals rather

than classes. Society is, for Sartre as for Marx, characterized by conflict, but this conflict is between individuals
rather than, or as well as, between classes. A universal
characteristic of individuals, as a result of the nature of
consciousness, is the desire to order the world in terms
of an individual project. One individual experiences
another as a competing organization of the world within
which his purposes and his self are reduced to the status
of objects. Relations between individuals are, therefore,
always characterized by conflict. "While I attempt to free
myself from the hold of the Other, the Other is trying to
free himself from mine; while I seek to enslave the Other,
the Other seeks to enslave me. . . . Conflict is the original meaning of being-for-others." [4] If this is accepted as
an accurate description of social relationships, antagonism between classes because of conflicting economic
interests would simply be a special instance, and not the
universal form, of social conflict. Two consequences
would ensue from Sartre's concept of class; classes
would lose their homogeneous quality, and conflict would
have to be expected in different forms even in a classless
society.

Sartre's view, while altering the perspective of the
class struggle, does not abolish it. Insofar as economically based social classes exist, the individuals in the
different classes will be in opposition. Class conflict is
the result of a will on the part of an underprivileged class
to change the existing social situation which is ordered
in accordance with the ideological preconceptions of the
privileged or dominant class. This will is essentially a
subjective movement within the individual members of
the lower class, and is conditioned but not determined
by the economic situation of the class. Both Sartre and
the Marxists refer to the will to change on the part of

the proletariat as class consciousness. Sartre has presented two different, though related, definitions of class consciousness. The first definition is given in *Being and Nothingness* in connection with his discussion of the Us-object as a dimension of interpersonal relations. It emphasizes the fact of conflict between individuals within the class combined with a sort of passive unity insofar as these individuals come under the gaze of a third party who considers them as object-members of a class.

> The primary fact is that the member of the oppressed collectivity, who as a simple person is engaged in fundamental conflicts with other members of this collectivity (love, hate, rivalry of interests, etc.), apprehends his condition and that of other members of this collectivity as looked-at and thought about by consciousnesses which escape him.[5]

According to this first definition of class consciousness the unity of a class stems from its members' experiences as objects before the gaze of the members of the dominant class, not from a community of economic interests. The proletariat thus becomes a creation of the social prejudices of the bourgeoisie. The bourgeois are responsible for determining the criteria of class membership, and the economic criteria which they employ are a function of their materialistic class values. The difference between the two classes is basically one of social status rather than the more narrow Marxist definition in terms of conflict of economic interests. The oppression suffered by the proletarian is not just economic deprivation but rather the experience of being a mere object, or means, in the world of another. Sartre does not seem to regard social class as merely an outgrowth of accidental prejudices. Wherever a social structure requires a hierarchical organization, with a resulting pattern of leaders and followers, the subject-object relationship between individuals becomes a functional part of the social system: ". . . a leader is never an object for his subordinates or he is lost; he is rarely a subject for his superiors." [6] Social organization, by canalizing the conflict between individuals, is instrumental in the creation of proletarian class consciousness.

The bourgeoisie, on the other hand, lacks consciousness of itself as a class, since its members are not objects in relation to the proletariat but rather subjects.

. . . the weakness of the oppressing class lies in the fact that although it has at its disposal precise and rigorous means for coercion, it is within itself profoundly anarchistic. . . . His [the bourgeois'] situation, in fact, does not allow him to apprehend himself as engaged in an Us-object in community with the other members of the bourgeois class. . . . It is only when the oppressed class by revolution or by a sudden increase of its power posits itself as "they-who-look-at" in the face of members of the oppressing class, it is only then that the oppressors experience themselves as "Us." [7]

The anarchy of the bourgeoisie prevents it from experiencing the social situation in terms of classes, with the result that its members fight among themselves and defend their economic interests on an individual basis; it is as if they already lived in a classless society. It does not seem that Sartre could share Marx's view of the capitalist class as dedicated to the defense of *class* interests insofar as such interests amounted to more than the sum of the interests of the individual members of the class. Marx's analysis of the behavior of social classes would be least true of the bourgeoisie, and most true of the proletariat, although primarily for reasons of social status rather than as a simple consequence of the economic structure. Race, nationality, and bureaucratic organizations, as well as social classes, can serve as the basis for the creation of Us-objects. Unities established on one of these bases may cross lines of conflict resulting from other divisions.

Sartre's second definition of class consciousness reflects a later development of his thought and is a corollary of his social ethics. He switches emphasis from the Us-object as a source of class unity to what might be termed the class as a moral community. The proletarian who accepts himself as an object is in bad faith, because while the experience of being an object for another is of prime importance, one can never be an object for oneself. The authentic proletarian will reject his being-as-object and actively pursue the goals of his own subjectivity. By doing so, he surpasses the passive suffering characteristic of the Us-object toward an ideal society in which he would be a free subject; i.e., a society ordered around his own values.

We recognize here Sartre's description of the revolutionary. Authentic class consciousness, given a revolutionary situation, is revolutionary class consciousness. The individual projects of the members of an oppressed class converge in a rejection of the social structure, as presently constituted, in the name of a future liberation. The unity of the class, or its consciousness of itself as a class, is identical with the actions of the class which are directed toward the realization of its social goals. Sartre rejects what he calls the "mechanical" definition of a class which presents a collection of like objects and not a unified whole; such a collection may exist but should properly be termed a "mass." In accordance with his doctrine of commitment, Sartre argues that the vision of a better future, which is equivalent to class consciousness, necessarily involves action toward the realization of that future, and that this in turn requires both a doctrine and an organization.

For this reason he believed that the welfare of the Communist Party in France carried with it the welfare of the French proletariat, since it was in fact their party. For describing the Communist Party as a necessary concomitant of proletarian class consciousness Sartre has been described as an "ultra-bolshevik" by Merleau-Ponty. Sartre disputes the validity of this accusation, but his contention that class consciousness is inseparable from action, and action from organization, indicates at least the distance which separates him from anarchism.

Sartre's second definition of class consciousness is to his first as a sociological fact apprehended authentically is to the same fact apprehended in bad faith. He contends that the second definition is consistent with Marx's doctrine of class consciousness, although he describes Engels as a mechanist-determinist on this point. However, his development of the concept of class consciousness is dependent upon a theory of human reality which has no counterpart in Marx's thought. Sartre does not hesitate to assert that the demand of a revolutionary is essentially a moral demand, made as a claim to a free life for the oppressed. Because of this, the proletarian view of society retains its subjective component, and cannot be considered as an entirely objective and thus definitive science of society as Marx tended to assume. Sartre's emphasis is on status rather than on economic power or income as the basis of social classes, and the picture which he presents of social class is less monistic than that of Marx. Their most serious disagreements arise on the subject of the classless society, which does not represent for Sartre a definitive solution of all social problems, but simply a state of society which will give rise to further projects of reform. Finally, Sartre presents a more complex picture than does Marx of the relation of human nature to social class. Sartre agrees that personality is a function of the social environment. He contends, however, that there are certain constants which characterize the human individual; they do not constitute a nature or personality, but nevertheless can serve as guides to human behavior within the context of a particular situation. In other words, as Marx believed, human nature can only be understood in terms of the social environment, but Sartre adds that it cannot be understood solely in terms of that environment. That which is universal is the human condition with its characteristics of individual responsibility, transcendence, freedom, etc.

Marx claimed that his doctrine differed from those of earlier socialist thinkers in that his approach was scientific whereas theirs had been utopian. Instead of formulating principles for the organization of an ideal society, he devoted himself to a realistic analysis of European society as it then existed. He was, however, just as indignant about the abuses which he discerned in the European social structure as the most idealistic of the utopian socialists. Because of his scientific orientation, and in accordance with his attack on moral systems as ideological, he was obliged to find a basis for criticism of what he felt to be social abuses. He found it in the concept of alienation, which had been originated by Hegel, and which can be defined broadly as a state of affairs in which the relation of the individual to the world, society, and to himself is inconsistent with his welfare as a personality and a human being. Other words sometimes used with substantially the same meaning are self-estrangement and depersonalization, and the symptoms felt by an alienated person are similar to those of schizophrenia. The individual cannot recognize his own purposes in the results of his efforts, and there is

a gulf between his intentions and the consequences of
the acts which are motivated by these intentions. Another way of describing an alienated person is to say
that the conduct required of a person by his social situation does not meet his emotional needs; human nature
is out of accord with the social system.

The particular form which Marx gave to this concept
was a description of man as alienated by the economic
system: in the attempt to provide for his material needs
man organizes himself for economic activity and sets in
motion a pattern of institutional development which results in dehumanizing conditions of work for the labor-
ing class, and a class system in which the worker is
robbed of the fruits of his own labor—the theory of
surplus value. The worker himself becomes a commodity
like any other object whose value is determined by
market conditions. The capitalist system thus appears as
inhuman, and the task to be achieved is the overthrow
of the existing social order and the establishment of a
classless society in which man's self-alienation will come
to an end. Marx apparently envisaged the classless society
as a society in which human relations would take spontaneous forms. The class system, the state, law, the family,
and ideology—in short, society as we know it—would
wither away and be replaced by natural and harmonious
social relationships. The defects in the Marxist diagnosis
and projected solution of the problem of alienation are
evident in their extremism; it seems highly unlikely that
changes in the mode of production could accomplish
such vast changes in man and his social relationships.

Sartre is as sensitive as Marx to the problem of alienation, but he differs as to its origin. The original sin is not
man's aim to produce the necessities of life, but the
existence of the Other. The problem of alienation is the

problem of the relation of the individual to society. The individual is alienated by being placed in a world where he is not free, in the sense of the free pursuit of the realization of his own ends. By looking at me the Other places me in a world which is alien to me. The worker who is paid for his labor is alienated because the purpose for which he is producing the article on which he works is not his own. "The alienating transcendence is here the consumer; that is, the 'They' whose projects the worker is limited to anticipating." [8] Even the ordinary experience of obeying directional signs in the subway or on the highway is a form of alienation, as is the use of a manufactured article; in following a sign or using a mass-produced article:

My immediate ends are the ends of the "They," and I apprehend myself as interchangeable with any one of my neighbors. In this sense we lose our real individuality, for the project which we are is precisely the project which others are.[9]

Alienation is far more pervasive for Sartre than it is for Marx, since it arises from the fact of social life, and not from one of its aspects, namely the mode of production. The individual can avoid this state of alienation only by assuming the determinations given him, by the look of the Other, the meanings inherent in his environment, and the techniques which he employs, as means to his own individual ends. Alienation is experienced by those individuals who are immersed in means and lose sight of ends, or accept their ends ready-made from an exterior source. Alienation is the result of attitudes in bad faith, and its cure is the assumption of freedom. Bad faith is essentially a flight from responsible action, which is the only way to give a subjective meaning to the objective determinations which threaten us with alienation.

Sartre's alternative to alienation is more somber than that of Marx, as it brings with it the anguish which results from a recognition of freedom. Also, there is no promise of a final historical resolution of the problem. Sartre's oppressed worker is a revolutionary, like that of Marx, but the revolution will not end all forms of alienation, and the classless society will be bearable to the individuals within it only if they in their turn surpass its determinations toward their own ends. If this seems a relatively somber hope, it stops short of the position of those other realists, the Christians, who tend to regard abuses as inevitable results of man's imperfections. Sartre resembles the Christian existentialists in his concern with alienation as a problem of individual subjectivity, and his call to the individual to leave the anonymity of the crowd for a consciousness of his individuality in the perspective of his transcendent goals. Because of his doctrine of commitment, however, he can disclaim the view that salvation is a purely individual, apolitical solution. Real community with others, which is necessary to escape from alienation, is possible only through identification with a dynamic process of social reform, or the elimination of social injustices. The transmuting of alienated social relationships into means toward individual goals cannot be achieved solely by the adjusting of inner attitudes; man is for Sartre an active animal, and possession of certain goals is inseparable from progress toward their realization. The belief in certain individual goals as normative without a concomitant effort to realize them on the social level by accepting the sometimes brutal necessities of political action characterizes the rebel, and is a form of flight into bad faith. To the degree that a particular social structure discourages by making difficult the effort of individuals actively to assert their own purposes, it encourages alienation and oppresses the individual. In this perspective public education which encourages conformity, and mass media which through distraction take from the individual his capacity for real experience, would seem no less oppressive than a secret police and arbitrary imprisonment if they were equally effective in alienating the individual.

Most of the Marxist replies to Sartre's criticisms of their doctrines can best be described as polemical; one Communist writer, for example, dismisses Sartre as a religious thinker who professes atheism in order to be in a better position to attack Communism. One hardly gets this impression from a reading of Sartre's works, unless concern for the moral dilemmas of individual life can be considered suitable only within the perspectives of traditional religious views. Sartre has dismissed as in bad faith the attacks upon him in the Communist organ *L'Humanité*, but has spoken with respect of two Marxists, Pierre Naville, a French Communist, and Georges Lukacs, a Hungarian. A rather lengthy statement of Naville is recorded in the discussion following Sartre's published lecture on existentialism, and Lukacs has written a book defending Marxism against the French existentialists, including Sartre. Lukacs' book is the most extensive and considered defense of Marxism against Sartre and may fairly be taken as representative of better quality Marxist thought on Sartrean existentialism.

Lukacs admits that Sartre's strictures against Marxists are to an extent justified. According to Lukacs, "vulgar" Marxists take economic determinism to mean a sort of mechanical relationship between the economic system and human consciousness, a point of view which neglects the role of human subjectivity in historical development:

. . . the emphasis on subjectivity constitutes the relatively justified element in existentialism. . . . It is a question, in effect, of underlining that it is men themselves who make their history, just as much in private life as in public affairs.[10]

Lukacs is, of course, entirely correct in attributing to Sartre a primary concern with the fact that history is made by men, and with the manner in which they make it. Sartrean existentialism is only relatively justified in Lukacs' eyes, however, because Marxism, as distinguished from the views of some Marxists, is global enough to include Sartre's emphasis on the creative role of the individual subject as well as an appreciation of the role of objective historical factors from which Sartre is excluded by his philosophy.

Within this perspective, Lukacs makes the following points: Marxism does not eliminate human subjectivity as a historically causative factor; existentialism neglects objective historical factors; and existentialism can be explained in terms of the attitudes of a particular social group at a particular time in history. Beginning with the first point, it appears that Sartre has not understood Marxism. The Marxist also holds that "man finds himself placed before a choice, face to face with a situation which requires resolution." The individual is free to break with the continuity of his life, and by willing and acting toward a new state of society may actually bring it about. At the same time, it is impossible within the framework of Marxism to hold a fatalistic view of historical development. Historical laws cannot be used to predict the future with the exactitude of those of astronomy. Since the course of objective historical development cannot be nicely calculated, only actions of individuals or groups can prove that the time for a revolution has arrived, for example, by successfully conducting such a revolution. In short, Lukacs denies that Marxism is guilty of mechanistic determinism in its interpretation of history and maintains that it gives an active role to individual subjectivity. His statement of the Marxist doctrine on the ability of reason to understand history resembles Gilson's statement of the Catholic position on the same question:

> . . . the whole of reality is always richer than the most adequate law . . . Positive law will never be more than the *approximation* of the real totality, always moving, constantly changing, infinite in every sense, which thought will never be able to describe perfectly.[11]

Because of this opacity of the real, humanity is called upon to create itself by its own efforts.

If these views, as Lukacs claims, can fairly be credited to the Marxists, it is easy to see why Lukacs refers to Sartre's emphasis on the creative role of the individual as "relatively justified" and claims that Sartre's attack on Marxism is misdirected. Before we conclude, however, that Sartre has not understood Marxism, some of the arguments which Lukacs advances to prove the superiority of Marxist materialism over what he terms Sartre's "idealism" must be examined. Because of Sartre's neglect of objective factors in nature and history, Lukacs contends, Sartre cannot give an adequate account of human nature, morality, or society. The weakest point in existentialism is its refusal to attribute a decisive role in the genesis of decisions made by individuals, and thus in the genesis of human nature, to the "reflection of objective reality in human consciousness." The individual is to be understood not in terms of a personal project but rather in terms of the degree to which he has assimilated the objective realities of his society. Individual behavior is a function of the social structure, and individuals differ in their degree of understanding, the accuracy of their perspective, and the profundity of their relation to social reality. Objective economic conditions are the real determinants of human nature. Instead of taking into consideration these conditions, the existentialists insist on an ahistorical, abstract "human condition":

> . . . categories such as being-together and being-in-the-world, . . . are, in effect, so abstract and so empty of all social content, that in starting from them one can deduce anything at all and even the contrary of anything at all.[12]

Pierre Naville also criticizes Sartre for overlooking the social and historical aspects of personality; he says that the "human nature" of early liberalism is actually closer to Marxism than the existentialist "human condition," because the older concept attempts to define man through generalizing about his actual historical behavior. This behavior can be usefully described in terms of the laws which govern it, but not in terms of an abstract "human condition." The Marxist point of view may be summed up as follows: the existentialists' view of human nature is vitiated by their insistence on the characteristics of subjectivity in terms of an extratemporal human essence rather than in relation to the social determinants of personality.

This argument of Lukacs does not seem to be decisive against Sartre's theory, whatever may be the case for that of the other existentialists. If Sartre refuses to employ the term *human nature*, it is because he is in agreement with the Marxists that man's essence must be understood in terms of his historical environment. If consciousness is for him an autonomous activity, it is still true that its contents are determined by or taken from the environment. The concrete reality for Sartre is not the human condition but the individual in a historical situation, or what he refers to as "man-in-the-world." It does not seem that Sartre cuts off the individual personality from its social roots as Lukacs claims, although it is true that Sartre discerns a suprahistorical human condition which is absent from Marxism in any explicit form. There is a real conflict here, however, which apparently lies at the source of Lukacs' inability to appreciate the importance of environmental determination in Sartre's theory of man. Lukacs expects much more from the environment than Sartre is willing to allow. According to Lukacs, there are objective laws of historical development which can be known approximately if not in detail, and action in accordance with the direction of historical development established by these laws is good.

In other words, virtue is the recognition of historical necessity, a point of view which is possible only on the assumption that objective historical forces carry progress within them, and this is an assumption which Lukacs criticizes Sartre for not making. In spite of Lukacs' reservations about the intelligibility of history, he himself seems to know where it is going: the only alternative to nihilism for modern man is socialism, the Soviet Union carries the future of socialism, capitalism will inevitably fall before socialism, the production of the material necessities of life is the "essential" activity of man, and complete knowledge of the good society is within reach.

The nonvulgar Marxism of Lukacs contains within it the same apparent inconsistency which characterizes the Catholic position. On the one hand the more sophisticated Marxists and Catholics assert that a rational grasp of human nature and social processes is impossible, while on the other hand they assert the indubitable nature and rational intelligibility of the laws of nature or history.

This apparent contradiction is rationalized by the concept of an absolute which reveals itself in different ways in different historical circumstances. The flux of history is difficult to grasp, but it contains the key to the absolute which governs it. Lukacs betrays an apparent ignorance of classical philosophy by asserting that "only dialectical materialism can arrive at this conception, at once supple and intransigent, of relativity as a moment of the absolute."

The danger that lies in the definition of an absolute is that it tends to be used as a fence to contain future individual or social development. Thus human nature is defined in such a way as to exclude divorce by the Catholics, and the laws of history are considered to require unconditional approval by the Communists of the policies of the Soviet government. In both cases the claim of an individual, to make his own decisions on matters which would seem well within the realm of historical relativity, is denied in the name of the absolute. At this point any concessions to the opacity of the historical moment amount to little more than an apologia for the mistakes of the hierarchy.

Sartre's objections to Marxism, of course, are directed against just this aspect of Marxist doctrine and what he regards as the philosophical errors responsible for it. He also sees an absolute in history, but it is the absolute of what he is fond of calling a "committed freedom," which is not subjected to a moral discipline but creates its own. Herbert Read has described as the greatest contribution of existentialism the view "that man is the reality—not even man in the abstract, but the human person, you and I; and that everything else—freedom, love, reason, God—is a contingency depending on the will of the individual." [13] Marxist materialism refuses to define human nature, but finds an essential development in history, the dialectic. Sartre also views human nature as contingent upon social reality, but describes the individual as transcending historical determinations by his freedom, which gives meaning and value to these determinations and permits the individual to make his own future.

According to Lukacs, no compromise is possible between Sartre's view and the Marxist conception of "the dialectical and historical unity of liberty and necessity, . . ." Whatever role the Marxists assign to human subjectivity, as materialists they are finally committed to the view that the individual is simply a product of a social system; the only form of transcendence possible is identification with the progressive forces in history. Sartre's view that freedom cannot express itself in terms of conforming to necessity seems to be psychologically more sound than the Marxist view, which imprisons individual subjectivity within a dogmatic rationalism.

In addition to defending Marxism against existentialism, Lukacs attacks existentialism on the grounds that it is not politically progressive, but on the contrary prepares the way for fascism. He states that Sartre himself does not have fascist tendencies, but that his progressive political views are inconsistent with his existentialist philosophy. The main defect of existentialist philosophy as the foundation for a political doctrine, from Lukacs' standpoint, seems to be its inability to take account of objective social forces. Marxism holds that knowledge of objective social reality and the equally objective laws which govern its development is not only possible but essential in the formation of a political program. Political intelligence is equivalent to a grasp of the direction of objective historical development. Existentialism, on the other hand, considers laws of history to be subjective in origin and probable in nature. Lukacs contends that the existentialist reduction of objective social development to the rank of the merely probable leads directly to moral nihilism. In order to understand his point of view it should be recalled that Marxism and existentialism are in agreement in rejecting suprahistorical moral absolutes. Marxism, however, asserts an objective standard for the evaluation of individual behavior: a good act is one which furthers rather than hinders the progress of history. When the existentialists deny the absolute character of laws of historical development, they abolish this moral standard. Sartre's moral requirement of respect for the liberty of the other is dismissed by Lukacs as a "Kantian" ethic which is contradicted by Sartre's existentialist philosophy.

Whatever may be said in criticism of Sartre's ethics, it does not seem fair to call him a nihilist even by implication. It is from the standpoint of Marxist ethics that existentialism appears to Lukacs to be a nihilism; the same accusation of nihilism can be made with equal justice against the Marxists by those who hold to suprahistorical absolutes as the basis for their ethical doctrines. Sartre's ethical doctrine has already been discussed; if it is not required by his ontology, it does not seem to be inconsistent with it. One could say of Lukacs' criticisms of existentialism what he says of Sartre's criticisms of Marxism: they are based on a misunderstanding of the doctrine.

The hardest part of existentialism for the rationalist to grasp is the fact that the "human condition" of the existentialists is *not* the essence of any particular man, nor is it in any sense a desirable goal to be attained. It is simply a perspective, whose result—at least in the case of Sartre's philosophy—is to emphasize the creative role of the individual personality, and the being of man as a process rather than as a static entity. If the existentialist says that life has no meaning but that which the individual brings to it, this does not mean that he believes that *his* life has no meaning. Lukacs fails to grasp this:

> The doctrine which teaches that life is particularly characterized by the lack of any perspective and that the sense of existence is completely inaccessible to knowledge is warmly welcomed by all those who think that their existence is deprived of any perspective and that their life makes no sense.[14]

Before leaving the dispute between Marxism and existentialism some notice should be taken of the very interesting analysis which Lukacs has made of the historical origins of existentialism. The non-Marxist is not necessarily accustomed to considering an explanation of the genesis of an idea as relevant to the question of its validity, but the identification of bourgeois origins for a philosophy is a Marxist way of proving it to be historically reactionary and therefore false. Lukacs classifies existentialism as a bourgeois philosophy of the decadent or imperialistic stage of capitalism. Existentialism resembles earlier bourgeois philosophy in its definition of reality in terms of the subjective attitudes of individuals, and in its "fetishism":

> . . . fetishism exerts an anti-dialectical effect on thought. More and more, society presents itself to bourgeois thought as a collection of dead things and relations between objects, instead of appraising it as it actually is, which is to say as the uninterrupted and constantly changing reproduction of human relationships.[15]

Existentialism appears as a modified form of idealism, which substitutes for reason the "cogito préréflexif" or

intuition, and its view of human reality is a universaliza-
tion of the plight of the bourgeois during the period of
the decline of capitalism.

Lukacs considers irrationalism and pessimism as the
two distinguishing characteristics of existentialism when
compared with earlier forms of bourgeois idealism. The
ideological function of irrationalism is to furnish an
escape from a situation where rationality would reveal
the decline of the class: that which is rational and in
conformity with the laws of historical evolution is condemned as inhuman, a condemnation which includes
both capitalism and socialism because both are creations
of man's rational capacities, while the irrational is glori-
fied as the properly human. This flight into irrationality
finds its methodological justification in the appearance
of irrationality resulting from the division of bourgeois
science into specialized systems whose concepts are not
interchangeable. The contradiction of discursive reason
in its attempts to describe reality poses a problem which
has the appearance of irrationality, but which Marxists
would resolve by a dialectical analysis of social evolution. The existentialists stop at the appearance of irrationality, and use it as the center of their system.
As for the pessimistic view taken by the existentialists
of the human condition, which is exemplified in Sartre's
identification of human consciousness with "nothingness,"
it is the feeling of a class condemned to death by history. Because of the close relationship between existentialism and the contemporary historical situation, existentialism will soon become the dominant spiritual
current among bourgeois intellectuals.

Lukacs' analysis leaves little doubt of how existentialists would be treated in those parts of the world where
Marxism is the official philosophy, and is well calculated

to discourage Marxists from existentialist leanings in spite of existentialism's relative justification in the eyes of our Marxist critic. The question of whether a faith in the rational intelligibility of historical evolution is more enlightened than a positive acceptance of the limitations of human knowledge remains unanswered, however. So does the question of whether a thoroughgoing optimism about man's ability to control history is more consistent with progressive politics than the mixture of pessimism and optimism offered by existentialism—if no better world is inevitable, neither are the particular evils of this one.

Sartre stands in direct opposition to the historical materialism which characterizes the Communist view of society, and attempts to substitute for the reduction of man to an object in the flow of world history a conception of man in society which gives its due to both the subjective and the objective aspect of human reality. In spite of his hostility toward the Marxist "myth," Sartre and the Marxists seem in many respects to talk the same language. This is partly due to the fact that both Marxism and existentialism represent reactions against the Hegelian system, while at the same time taking over some of the Hegelian terminology and concepts. More important, however, in explaining the kinship between Sartre and the Marxists are, in the first place, the prominent role which Marx played in the genesis of modern European sociology and, in the second place, the congruence between certain aspects of the social analyses of Marx and of the existentialists.

Even in the United States, the contributions of Marx are most likely to be stressed today by sociologists, in spite of the fact that in most cases such concepts as social classes and society as a functional system were not taken originally from him but developed separately in this country. One can thus speak of a rehabilitation of Marx by modern social scientists, although the extent to which this is likely to go is sharply limited by the attitudes stemming from the cold war. French social scientists make far greater use of Marxist terminology and concepts, and their filiation to Marx is frequently both direct and explicit. This is particularly true of those whose political sympathies lie to the left, as Marx is the patron saint of the socialist parties as well as of the Communists. This does not mean, of course, that the French social scientists are any more committed to the philosophy of dialectical materialism than are the American, but simply that they accept Marx as one prominent social scientist whose ideas are subject to the same criticism in the light of recent research as those of any other writer in the field. What is involved here is essentially the fact that the categories and observations of Marx are more in line with those of contemporary social science than is the case for either liberalism or Catholicism. Consequently, it should occasion no surprise when Sartre, as he sometimes has done, refers to himself as a Marxist, and this is no indication of affiliation with the Communists or admiration for their doctrine.

Finally, there are those aspects of Marx's thought which figure as anticipations of some of the major emphases of existentialist philosophy. Marx also attacked attempts to give a final definition of man by abstract theorizing, and pointed to the roots of such philosophies in the historical period in which they were produced. His concept of ideology revealed how social doctrines functioned as rationalizations for the unconscious motives of particular social classes. Freud and the existentialists also emphasize the ideological character of idea systems, and search for the roots of ideas in the life situation of those who hold them. Likewise, there is agreement on the alternative to abstract theorizing as a method of contact with reality, namely, the view that knowledge of reality is derived from activity. The existentialist concern with truth as a revelation of lived experience, of action, is similar to Marx's emphasis on acting upon society as the means of acquiring knowledge of it. Finally, the concept of alienation, of the estrangement of man from himself, is of central importance in both Marxism and existentialism. In his discussions of these subjects Marx concentrated upon the area of political economy, and particularly the capitalist system. Sartre provides a more detailed and systematic account of the role of human subjectivity in knowing, and extends his study of alienation to include, for example, man in the Soviet Union.

An Existentialist in Politics

It is clear that Sartre is critical of the important ideologies of his time because he feels that they do not give an adequate role to individual freedom, and even encourage in their followers a flight from freedom into bad faith. His positive contribution to social theory would thus seem to lie in a reformulation of the concept of freedom: ". . . everything which resembles closely or distantly existentialism . . . is a problem of freedom . . ." [1] Sartre's discussion of freedom is, however, not always as clear as might be expected. It would be easy, if not very informative, to assemble a series of quotations from his works on the subject which would appear to be confused and contradictory. For example, he says in one place that man wants freedom, and in another that man is condemned to be free. The only way to understand his various uses of the term is to review briefly his theory of human reality and his political doctrine with special reference to the problem of freedom.

The clearest expression of Sartre's concept of freedom is contained in his essay on Descartes. In this essay Sartre distinguishes two theories of freedom held by Descartes, one of which might be termed freedom-autonomy and the other freedom-conformity. Freedom as autonomy is a condition of the Cartesian method: Descartes thought it possible to doubt everything, save the fact that he doubted. Now, to doubt is to will not to accept ideas conceived by the understanding. By a subsequent movement, it is possible to accept certain ideas and not others. A being who determines his own understanding creates his own world; that is, he is autonomous. Descartes' second theory of freedom defines man's freedom as his ability to identify himself with absolute truth. Descartes himself credits the first type of freedom to God, the second to man. Sartre credits Descartes with profound insight into the nature of freedom on the basis of his theory of freedom as autonomy:

Descartes understood perfectly that the concept of freedom involved the requirement of an absolute autonomy, that a free act was an absolutely new production whose germ could not be contained in a previous state of the world and that, consequently, freedom and creation are two terms for the same thing. Freedom . . . is pure productivity, it is the extra-temporal and eternal act by which . . . there is a world, a Good and eternal Truths. . . . the root of all reason is to be sought in the depths of the free act, it is freedom which is the foundation of the true, and the rigorous necessity which appears in the order of truths is itself maintained by the absolute contingency of the free creative will, and this dogmatic rationalist could say, with Goethe, not: "In the beginning was the Word," but: "In the beginning was the Act." [2]

This theory of freedom as autonomy, for Descartes a description of the freedom of God, is Sartre's concept of human freedom:

It would require two centuries of crisis—crisis of Faith, crisis of Science—for man to recover this creative liberty which Descartes found in God and for one to finally suspect this truth, the essential basis of humanism: man is the being whose appearance causes a world to exist.[3]

Descartes' other theory of freedom, which is close to the traditional Catholic doctrine that man is free to conform to his essence—which is pre-established by God—or to refuse this essence and choose nonbeing, Sartre credits to the Catholic dogmatism imposed upon Descartes by the ideological climate of the seventeenth century. The doctrine of freedom-conformity appears, in a different form, in Marxism, which defines freedom as the recognition of historical necessity. It also typifies a certain type of liberalism, for which freedom demands only social recognition of the rights which are prescribed by natural law. In each case man is considered free in conforming to an order independent of his will, and the only purely individual act which he can perform is to defy the order. Defiance is an autonomous act but not creative, since it leaves the pre-established order intact. For example, one could say that the music composed by Mozart of his own inspiration would be of poor quality, and that his genius lay in discovering music already laid up in heaven. It may be plausible to describe Mozart's music in this fashion, but it is doubtful that he himself composed according to the theory. Sartre describes the perspective of those who follow this theory in the realm of morals:

God, through the agency of the natural and supernatural enlightenment which he dispenses to them, conducts them by the hand toward the Knowledge and the Virtue which he has chosen for them; they have only to let themselves go; all the merit for this progress returns to him. But, to the degree that they are nothingness, they escape him; they are free to let go of his hand on the journey and to plunge into the world of sin and non-being. On the other hand, naturally, they can always guard themselves from intellectual and moral evil: guard themselves, protect themselves, suspend judgment, repress desires, stop actions in time. They are only asked, in short, not to interfere with the plans of God.[4]

To this he opposes, in the words of Descartes, the perspective of the autonomous individual:

I believe that true generosity, that which causes a man to esteem himself as highly as it is permissible to esteem oneself, consists only partly in knowing that the only thing which really belongs to one is the free disposition of his will, and that one must be praised or blamed according to whether he uses it well or poorly, and partly in feeling in oneself a firm and constant resolution to use it well, which is to say never to lack the will for undertaking and executing all the things which he will judge to be the best: which is to follow perfect virtue.[5]

The theory of liberty as autonomy which Sartre credits to Descartes and claims as his own is more than consistent with his philosophical system—it is at the heart of it. Without repeating the earlier analysis of Sartre's ontology, brief reference can be made to some of the elements which support this concept of freedom. Since human consciousness is nothingness, it cannot contain its own motives, and since it acts by negation, it cannot be determined by any exterior influence. Thus arises the necessity for man to choose freely his own motivations, an event which Sartre refers to as the original choice. This original choice is the basis of both truth and value as far as that individual is concerned, and determines both his view of the world and his nature or essence. The freedom of the original choice appears in the possibility of its being changed, a change which would stem from a radically new decision. Such a change would be exceptional, since it could not be motivated by the original choice; it is best described as a conversion experience. Through the free choice of his motives, the individual presents us always with something which cannot be reduced to environmental determination or an inner human nature, and this is the organizational principle of his life. This freedom, or autonomy, is the source of the moral dignity of the individual, since by creating himself he creates one possible image of man.

A peculiarity of Sartre's theory of freedom, which differentiates it from other doctrines of free will, is the fact that man chooses himself all at once, so to speak, by the choice of an ultimate goal which thereafter constitutes the particular motives for his daily acts. Change or development for an individual is normally the result of striving to reach this future state, rather than a new choice of oneself. Sartre's free choice thus resembles Freudian psychological determinism, rather than "free will" in the sense of deliberate choice as a result of a process of reflection. Sartre's view is consistent with the existentialist emphasis on the whole man, rather than on man as a rational animal, and constitutes a rehabilitation of emotional life. It has been considered, however, inconsistent with the moral responsibility of the individual and thus without value for establishing the dignity of the individual. If the daily acts of an individual are determined, then moral deliberation is a farce, and Sartre means something radically different by freedom than, for example, Descartes. A freedom of this sort, which is the factual condition of all men regardless of their circumstances or behavior, would seem to be politically and morally irrelevant.

Sartre does not believe this to be the case, however. Freedom as a part of the human condition is a necessary precondition for the choice of freedom as a way of life on the reflective level. It is, however, not a sufficient condition. Sartre envisages two possible reactions to the condition of freedom: the acceptance or choice of freedom as the highest value, and the flight from freedom or bad faith. The choice of freedom as the foundation of all value is characteristic of the authentic individual, who chooses to act as if he were free, which of course according to Sartre's theory he in fact is. In other words, the authentic individual chooses to live the human condition. Since the consciousness of choosing freely carries with it anguish, there is a constant motive for an illusory escape into bad faith. Sartre is not embarrassed by the minor role which he gives to free will in the usual sense. The choice of freedom means to him fidelity to self, or radical orientation toward a future defined by the individual's chosen goal, and a constant sense of responsibility for choices made. Freedom is something to be achieved, as well as a part of the human condition. One cannot speak of freedom as the essence of man in general, but rather as a possibility for all men.

It can be said at this point that Sartre gives an intelligible account of human freedom, and that a corollary of this freedom is the moral dignity of the individual because of his moral creativity and personal responsibility. The authentic individual who chooses to live his freedom acquires in Sartre's political thought something of the aura of the proletariat in Marxism, and for a similar reason: it is the free action of the individual which bears within it a more humane future for man. Progress in history is identical with the progress of free individuals in the realization of their projects. It is for this reason that Sartre deplores the prevalence of political ideologies which hide from us the nature of the contribution we must make to the achievement of a more just society. Sartre's description of human reality as free, and his moral requirement that man choose freedom as the highest value, because it is the source of all values, put him necessarily in opposition to any ideology which

subjects human freedom to the realization of any particular social or political order.

This does not mean that Sartre aligns himself against
political change. On the contrary, the authentic individual has been described by Sartre as a revolutionary. The
argument that the existentialist must be a revolutionary
is based upon two elements in Sartre's description of
human reality. Here again, the authentic individual
simply wills to live the human condition as it actually
is. The first fact which he wills to accept is the organization of his activity around the achievement of his project.
His life takes on the characteristic of a constant striving
toward the morally valuable end set by his freely chosen
project. The status quo appears only as something to be
surpassed. It has been remarked that Sartre's theory
would require revolution even against a free society,
supposing that such a society were in fact attained. It
is of course true that Sartre envisages "permanent revolution"; there is no reason to suppose that the rejection
of the status quo in the name of a more valuable future
would disappear in any society, since it is a part of
the universal human condition. On the other hand, the
temptation to escape from freedom into bad faith, with
its concomitant of interpersonal conflict, and the lack of
any blueprint for an ideal society would make it very
unlikely that a perfect society could ever become a historical reality. Further, it must be borne in mind that
Sartre's use of the term "revolution" is somewhat particular. Whether the authentic individual would be a
revolutionary, in the sense of working toward the violent
overthrow of the constituted authorities, is determined
by his situation. Lacking a revolutionary situation, the
authentic individual would be what is more commonly

termed a reformist. Sartre's definition of the term "revolutionary" does not hinge on the degree of violence, but
rather on the determination to effect social reforms by
political means.

The second fact which the authentic individual wills
to accept is the equivalence between the realization of
his project and the achievement of social change. This
equivalence is a result of Sartre's ontology; human consciousness, which by separating man from the determinations of being-in-itself is the source of his freedom,
is not something other than being-in-itself but a nothingness which reveals being. It manifests itself as a particular organization and evaluation of the environment,
not as something other than the environment. That is why
Sartre describes man as a freedom-in-situation, and this
description serves as the ontological foundation of his
view of man as a political animal. The self-realization of
the individual is seen as necessitating reform of society
in accordance with his values. Man is political, however, rather than just social, because of the nature of
interpersonal relations. We have already seen that respect
for the freedom of others is a moral requirement of
authenticity. At the same time, because of the conflict
which according to his doctrine characterizes interpersonal relations, Sartre has stated that respect for the
freedom of others is impossible. Not only the use of
violence, but even education and tolerance involve violation of the freedom of the other because they determine his situation and hence his possibilities. Violation
of the freedom of others is thus an inevitable aspect of
social life and of social reform regardless of the means
employed. The contradiction between the moral requirement of respect for the freedom of the other and the
impossibility of such a respect in fact is not resolved but

rather assumed by the authentic individual, who justifies the inevitable violation of the freedom of some others in the name of a greater freedom for all. Thus government and politics, with their concomitant of violence, are the inevitable consequence of the conflict which characterizes social life and are relatively justified. Good government and desirable policies are the fruit of respect by the authorities for freedom, and their efforts to advance it. By the same token the authentic individual engages in political action aimed at serving the cause of freedom.

No particular form of government or particular policy can be considered always and everywhere the best, since different forms of government may be suitable to the advancement of freedom under different circumstances. Sartre seems to think that political democracy based upon universal suffrage is peculiarly suited to a free society, since its foundation is the equal ability of each citizen to choose himself by choosing his political regime. Nevertheless, he could approve an authoritarian regime when the nature of the political task to be accomplished seemed to require it, since democracy is a means to individual freedom and not an end in itself. All governments bear within them a tendency toward suppression of individual freedom, because institutional organization requires leaders who tend to look on their followers as objects rather than as free subjects.

Going from the role of the state in Sartre's existentialist political thought to the relationship between the individual and the state, we find that he relies upon the concept of freedom as a standard for political organization. Since all individuals are in fact free, they are all in fact equal. This equality is moral, and has as its chief effect the requirement that the freedom of all be equally respected. The authentic individual seeks the liberation of all men,

not of a particular group. Sartre also adopts the concept
of fraternity: the individual requires a sense of participation in a joint enterprise. Sartre's phrase for the unity
which he regards as essential is recognition of the freedom of others. As the affirmation of one's freedom is
inseparable from political action, so the recognition of the
freedom of others is more than an inner attitude. It is participation in a common effort aimed at remedying social
injustice. Finally, as might be expected, the individual
requires personal liberty. Sartre's discussion of this matter
can be confusing to the casual reader, for he uses the
French word *liberté* to mean both freedom and liberty.
There is an apparent confusion in combining the statements that man is free and that he must be made free.
Only when used in the latter sense can man's freedom be
considered as a limit on state action. The confusion disappears if a distinction is made between freedom and
the power of the individual to act in certain ways. That
Sartre is not confused on this point is indicated by the
fact that he distinguishes between these two meanings of
liberté.[6]

Personal liberty as a requirement means the existence
for the individual of a field of action which will permit
him to pursue his individual project. In other words, the
individual can claim those liberties which are essential to
his self-realization. This traditional language should not
obscure the fact that Sartre gives a particular meaning
to self-realization, which although not necessarily peculiar to him is nevertheless closely connected with his
philosophy. Sartre asserts that man is a totality, by which
he means that his freedom manifests itself in all aspects
of his life, and therefore in all his relationships with
society. Consequently, self-realization involves, for example, economic as well as political rights. Also, self-

realization is not just a process of inner development, although it involves inner development, but action upon society. In addition to action, the pursuit of the individual project also involves possession. A major form of self-realization is the appropriation of things in order that they may be *my* things. Property is an extension of the personality into the world, and in addition functions as a defense against others by giving each person his own private world. Property is thus more than a social convention; it is a means of self-realization. Sartre has nowhere pointed out the connection of this aspect of his ontology with his political views. It appears, however, that he would admit both possession and action as claims of the individual, subject to limitation on the basis of respect for the freedom of the other. If the liberties required for individual self-realization are incompatible with the existing social order, the authentic individual will be a revolutionary. Reformist or revolutionary, the authentic individual sees the future in terms of progress. Progress is not inevitable, however; it demands effort and offers only a possible reward. And it remains in the domain of the relative, since it appears as a response to the abuses of a particular social order.

This brief summary of some of the more important parts of Sartre's political theory is intended to draw together some of the discussions of his political views contained in earlier chapters, and to show the relationship between these views and his description of human reality. Sartre's theory of politics resembles his doctrine of the human condition, in that both deal with the universal structures of history and are intended to furnish a perspective within which individual historical phenomena can be understood. That is, just as individual behavior cannot be explained by the human condition but only by a particular project and set of experiences, so a political regime requires explanation in terms of the political ideology and historical circumstances which it expresses. Similarly, Sartre's political doctrine does not furnish a particular line of political action, since the values which preside over such action are historical, the product of individual actions, and not of his ontology or ethics. What it offers is a call to political action, a justification for social change, a demand for tolerance of individual nonconformity, and an assertion of the primacy of the moral purposes of the community over its institutional structure. The nature of the political action, the particular social changes to be accomplished, the limits of nonconformity, and the values capable of providing unity are determined by the spontaneous activity of individuals within a given social situation. As man is a moral being who creates values, so he is a political being who realizes utopias.

Sartre has given us an example of what he understands by existential commitment in politics in his own political activities from the Second World War to the present. During the occupation of France by the Germans, and after his release from a German concentration camp for reasons of health, he took part in the Resistance, writing articles for clandestine publications and forming an action group. During this period, political activity in the ordinary sense was impossible, since Paris was under the control of the occupying authorities. The Resistance was, as Sartre himself has said, purely an individual solution: it was impossible to plan for the future, since the outcome of the War was in doubt and the Resistance could not hope to prevail by itself against the Germans. The unity of Frenchmen of all political tendencies, including the Communists, and the great sacrifice of each individual to the ideal of freedom, led to great hopes for the regeneration of France if and when liberation finally came.

After the Allies had liberated Paris he contributed articles on the postwar situation to the newspaper *Combat,* for which Albert Camus also wrote. This newspaper was the voice of the intellectuals active in the Resistance who advocated important political and social changes that would cure France of the weaknesses which had characterized the Third Republic. On October 1, 1945, the first issue of *Temps Modernes* appeared, a monthly journal dedicated to clarifying the political issues of the postwar world. Its editorial committee included, in addition to Sartre, Simone de Beauvoir, Raymond Aron, and Maurice Merleau-Ponty, to mention only those best known in the United States. It represented the intellectual left, and was devoted to critical analyses of the policies of the United States and the Communist world, as well as assessments of the French political situation and a decreasing number of purely literary efforts. This enterprise reflected Sartre's belief, a product of his philosophy, that writers have a responsibility for their society, and that the function of literature is to present the reader with the author's view of social reality. Some of the policies advocated in this publication included opposition to the Western Defense Community, to the wars in Indo-China and Algeria, and to German rearmament, and support for democratic liberties in France and for socialism. A series of disagreements on political matters resulted in a number of well-publicized divisions among the sponsors of *Temps Modernes,* until Sartre and Mme. de Beauvoir alone remained of the group mentioned above.

In 1949, Sartre, David Rousset, and others of a similar political persuasion attempted the formation of a political party, the Democratic Republican Rally, which was to provide a nondoctrinaire alternative to those dissatisfied with the other leftist parties. It was to be a party of reform and more democratic in its internal organization than the other parties, notably the Communist Party. This effort inspired considerable enthusiasm among the intellectuals but failed to acquire mass support and soon dissolved. From this failure Sartre drew the lesson that the left could not progress in France without the collaboration of the Communists, and he proceeded to set an example, in his writings and his actions, for a unified left. Praising the expressed objectives of the Communist Party in France, and condemning the red-baiting which was fostered by the cold war atmosphere, he defended the Party on many occasions, notably in his series of three articles on "Communism and Peace" which were published in *Temps Modernes* beginning in 1952. He also attended and praised the Communist Peoples' Peace Congress in Vienna at about the same time. During the period of Sartre's attempt to find a basis for co-operation with the Communists, he continued to criticize the rigidity and stagnation of the French Communist Party and reiterated his refusal to become a Party member. This period came to an end in 1957 when, again in *Temps Modernes,* he attacked as inexcusable the Soviet repression of the Hungarian revolt, and gave up his adopted role as a sympathetic critic of the Communist Party.

If Sartre's attitude toward the Communists has justified his being described as a fellow traveler, it must be noted that he innovated in the role. The term fellow traveler usually is used to describe a person who shares the Communist philosophy while lacking the courage to participate in Party activities. Sartre rejected the Communist philosophy but defended the party publicly in a way which led to his being attacked from all quarters, including the Communists themselves. Sartre's estimation of the nature of the French political scene has been frequently attacked, as has his apparent presumption in thinking that his own actions might have some effect on political realities: for example, in persuading the Communists to co-operate with the non-Communist left. In his defense of his position Sartre tended to describe society as a product of freely chosen individual attitudes in the face of responsibilities. This is a moral view of society, and he thought the task of the political analyst to be the apportionment of praise or blame to individuals and groups insofar as their attitudes adhere to or deviate from the standard of respect for the moral integrity of the individual. Thus Sartre's approval "in principle" of Communism, on the grounds that its declared intention is the construction of democratic socialism.

This picture of political events as the product of individual wills ignores the question whether or not a particular political action and the attitude which supposedly underlies it are, in the light of the objective factors of historical development, supported by the actual trend of history. It might well be, for example, that French Communism will eventually appear to have been a road block rather than a steppingstone in the path toward a more just social order in France. Sartre's philosophy does not necessarily preclude consideration of objective factors in historical development. The fact that man is always in situation and achieves his goals only through engagement would seem to require consideration of such factors. Moreover, even the original choice, the source of individual moral standards, has historical content, because it is the choice of a certain relation to society and the world. Finally, our social being which is the means to the realization of our project is a function of the projects of others which in turn take their content from the situations of others. So far, however, these aspects of Sartre's philosophy have taken second place in Sartre's political analyses to the view, likewise a product of his philosophy, that reform involves a free surpassing of the social context toward an ideal goal which is set by the standard of freedom for all. The future appears as the free creation of individual wills; the future of socialism will not be served by history but by the creative action of the Communist Party. The verdict of history lies not in the impersonal action of objective historical forces but in the "look" of future generations. Man makes his own history.

The connection between this voluntaristic view of history and Sartre's philosophy is obvious. Man invents mankind, and in so doing makes history. It is also obvious to what degree this view sacrifices political realism—history is as much a record of the frustration of men's purposes as of their realization. Burke, in emphasizing the limited possibilities of political reform, was more intelligent than this. So was Marx, who tied political success to objective economic developments. There is no question that Sartre does give less importance to the determining influence of traditions and of economic institutions by emphasizing the subjective element in history. There is also no question that political analysis cannot afford to neglect the objective element—the peculiar mixture of rationalism and irrationalism in fascism would seem to furnish the best example of a political movement based on voluntarism and pure creation.

Sartre is, however, no fascist. Since he presents himself as violently anti-fascist, it might be better to say that Sartre's political analyses do not furnish fascism with a

political theory. This is because Sartre does not accept
the doctrine that the end justifies the means. Instead, he
sees ends and means as in a precarious balance which
must be struck in terms of the effects of a policy on
presently existing individuals. Since there is no absolute
justification for any particular present action which requires treating individuals as objects and therefore carries a certain amount of human degradation, each step
in the name of human freedom must find its justification
in the actual advancement of the freedom of existing
individuals. Sartre was in effect willing to give the Communists a superiority in principle over other political
parties, but reserved judgment as to actual policies of
the Party. In his discussion of the Hungarian revolt of
1956 he contends that the very superiority in principle
requires the application of more exacting standards of
judgment as to the policies followed, and concludes that
no eventual triumph of socialism can justify the harm
done to the socialist cause by the slaughter of Hungarian
workers.

Furthermore, Sartre contends that every revolt is
against specific historical abuses, that the suppression of
a particular injustice will only reveal others, and that
consequently the necessity of reform will probably never
be outmoded by the realization of an ideal society. Historical progress is only piecemeal and relative. If those
writers are correct who trace the roots of totalitarianism
to a demand for the historical realization of a utopia,
to the "immanentization of the eschaton," [7] then Sartre
would seem to be cleared of any charge of totalitarian
tendencies. Sartre's insistence on the limitations of political action is a result of his skepticism as to the bases for
the traditional utopias, and as to the limitations inherent in individual endeavor. There is no perfect order

in the mind of God, or inherent in the nature of man, or within the vision of the social sciences, or at the term of historical development. An individual can project such an order, but his vision is partial and his time is short. He can have no certainty that others will continue his work. Sartre shares with other existentialists, and with religious thinkers such as Reinhold Niebuhr, a sense of the tragedy and ambiguity of action in history.

The reasons for Sartre's emphasis on the subjective side of historical development in his writings on contemporary political questions would not seem to be altogether inherent in his philosophy. They result rather from his situation as a writer. Historical knowledge, according to Sartre, is only probable, and social science is in its infancy. Therefore the calculation of the future effects of the evolution of objective historical factors is problematical at best. In the meantime Sartre, as an intellectual who because of his success finds himself in the public eye, must take a stand on every issue. He is obliged to act since, as he has frequently pointed out, even silence is action in support of the existing order of things, and his philosophy requires him to be the spokesman for a more just social order. The positions which he has consequently taken, as for example his arguments in favor of the Communist Party, may be challenged, but the moral fervor which inspires his pronouncements is beyond question. The attempt to recall his readers to their moral responsibility in facing an issue is a constant feature of all his writings. In addition he regularly attempts to clarify concepts, define issues in a manner to give them reality, and to destroy patterns of doctrinal mystification. His articles are constantly recalling his readers to their duty to think for themselves. As for his political opinions, he has stated that:

The fact of being on the side of certain people, of taking the part of the Rosenbergs or declaring myself opposed to the rearmament of Germany, implies only my own commitment as a man and writer. I am incompetent on the level of technical political action. Politics, insofar as it concerns me, is limited to the use I make of my ballot.[8]

Sartre and the Ideologies

CHAPTER XI

It is difficult to tell whether the second half of the twentieth century will see an increase or a decrease in the importance of ideology. On the one hand, the Second World War seemed to announce an era of conflict among secular religions, each one claiming to have a monopoly on the path to earthly salvation, which cut across and thus rendered relatively impotent the old nationalisms, so long considered a cause of international strife. At the present time, in some of the most powerful regions of the world, there seems to be a contrary trend toward the replacement of idealists by manipulators, administrators, and technologists in the positions of power, and a decline of militancy among populations which are increasingly concerned with the immediate satisfaction of their private desires for material things. It does not seem that this latter trend will spread to the new nations of Asia for some time, however, because of the vast distance between them and even a relative prosperity. As for the nations which are more economically advanced, ideology remains a potent factor, capable of rallying support for "freedom" against "Communist slavery" or for "socialism" against "predatory capitalism." In France the conflict of ideologies exists not merely on the international level but also as a domestic problem, which accounts for the importance given by Sartre to the attitudes, ideas, and philosophies connected with them.

It is not difficult to discern a pattern in Sartre's criticisms of political ideologies. A fundamental defect shared by Catholicism, liberalism, and Marxism is their ascription of a final rationality to the natural and social order which Sartre considers methodologically unjustified. They oppose the ignorant and imperfect individual to the massive certainty of the universe, which operates in terms of laws that are both rational and right. To this view of the world Sartre contrasts the "absurd" universe of the existentialists, a universe devoid of human significance. This concept of the absurdity of the world appears in Sartre's literary work as a revelation of the experience of nausea, and in his philosophy as a characteristic of his description of the *en-soi,* or being-in-itself. It is also implicit in the experience of anguish, which is a concomitant of existential choice, or choice in the knowledge of right and wrong but without any sure guide to right action.

The vision of the world as absurd has frequently been traced, as for example by the Marxists, to the experience of a particular social group at a particular time in history, although the definition of the group varies with the commentator. In addition to the irrelevance of this type of argument with regard to the truth or falsity of the existentialist position, it would seem that, in the world of the intercontinental rocket and the atomic bomb, the assumption of a beneficent destiny in a friendly world will be questioned by other than the French intellectuals, the European bourgeoisie, or even western Europeans in general. Furthermore, explanation of the existentialist world view in sociological terms tends to obscure its more properly philosophic origins. In the first place, the use by natural science in "explaining" the world of mathematically formulated hypotheses subject to empirical verification has deprived the doctrine of natural law of any claim to a scientific foundation. In the second place, the epistemological analysis of Hume, with its separation of reason, fact, and value, has revealed the methodological fallacies involved in ascribing rationality to nature or in attempting to prove ultimate values by operating according to the laws of formal reasoning. Finally, the discovery of the effects of ideological bias on social science and the resulting concept of a value-free sociology and political science establishes the same relationship between man and history as the natural sciences had established between man and the cosmos.

The absurdity of the world is equivalent, in this context, to the indifference of the world and history to human reason and values. Evaluation is a characteristic of a free human subjectivity, and things are not valuable in themselves. Insofar as this is the meaning of the absurdity of the world to the existentialists, existentialism is a parallel position to positivism. The positivists, however, react to this view of the world by concentrating their attention on scientific analysis, excluding matters of evaluation from rational enquiry, while the existentialists relegate scientific knowledge to a secondary status and regard as primary the evaluative aspects of human experience. When this point of view is pushed to an extreme, the world becomes hostile and threatening, science a diversionary activity or a pseudo-knowledge, and reason a trap rather than a guide. What is left is a kind of introverted mysticism, which emphasizes the adoption of a religious attitude and offers no clear guide to action. This type of existentialism justifies references to the "basic anti-objectivistic attitude of modern existential

philosophy," [1] and leads to the charge that existentialism
is irrelevant to social and political problems.

Whatever may be the case for other existentialists, it
does not seem that Sartre draws these conclusions from
the absurdity of the world. He seems to view the world,
and history, as something to be salvaged rather than
ignored. He has spoken eloquently and at length in favor
of the economically underprivileged and the social out-
cast, and against anti-Semitism and the torture of Algerian
prisoners by the French Army. His discussions of such
difficult subjects for a Frenchman as collaborators and
the occupying German Army in France are a model of
fairness and restraint. Sartre's concern with social and
political problems indicates that, on the practical level,
his existentialism does not lead to withdrawal. It might
be said that this activism is traditional for French intellectuals regardless of their philosophical persuasion.
Sartre would be acting like a French intellectual, and not
particularly like an existentialist. Also, the life of a
philosopher need not bear any more conclusive relationship to his ideas than his social class. Nevertheless, Sartre
doubtless regards his philosophy as supplying mandates
for action, and his essays on political and social matters,
like his literary works, can be fully understood only
within the perspective of his philosophy. Perhaps there
is some justification in taking the philosopher's life as
evidence of the content of his philosophy in the case of
an existentialist, since existentialism has since Kierkegaard
had as its primary goal the supplying of the individual
with a guide to life by making philosophy the servant of
the full scope of individual demands on life. Philosophy
for the true existentialist is not a discipline among other
disciplines, but a vocation.

However, any attempt to explain Sartre's concept of

the absurd, which at once marks him as an existentialist and furnishes the basis for his criticisms of political ideologies, must go beyond the testimony of his personal life and into the content of his philosophy. The fact that he holds such a concept, that he denies the accessibility to science or philosophy of a rational-normative world order, hardly requires demonstration at this point. The question to be answered is rather the role which the concept plays in his system, and its implications for his political thought.

Absurdity is a relational concept; something appears to be absurd when it is at variance with the expectations of an observer, whether these expectations are based upon reason or prejudice. The necessary duality which makes possible absurdity occurs in Sartre's philosophy as the concepts of being-in-itself and being-for-itself, or nothingness. Being-in-itself, considered objectively, lacks both purpose and order. It is present as a meaningless plenitude. Being-for-itself, on the other hand, is purposive: its purpose is its freely chosen project. Rationality is subordinate to this purpose, since reason is governed by the purposes inherent in the project. Absurdity appears as a characteristic of being-in-itself when grasped by the being-for-itself as indifferent to its purposes, and therefore irrational. It is easy to recognize here the existentialist view of the isolated, forlorn individual in a hostile world. This is for Sartre a part of the human condition, a universal characteristic of man; man is also a striving toward the goals which are set by his project. Since his perception of the world is in terms of his project, which gives to things a coefficient of advantage or adversity, he does not ordinarily see the world as absurd, but rather as ordered around his ends. The experience of absurdity, of anguish or nausea, is exceptional. Rocquentin, the "hero" of Sartre's novel *Nausea*, is a bachelor, an intellectual, solitary in his habits, without a steady employment, and in a strange town. Sartre has never held that nausea is a way of life; his authentic individual does not contemplate the absurdity of the world but actively pursues his chosen ends. The absurdity of the world is, however, a fact. Its practical significance is in the consequent impossibility of any value system being inherent in a "natural" order apart from the will of the individual. In short, the knowledge of the absurdity of the world makes the individual responsible for his actions in pursuit of the ends which are, he knows, worthy only because he has chosen them to be such. The denial of the absurdity of the world has as its immediate consequence the opening up of an avenue of escape from the responsibility of an individual for his actions. Thus the absurdity of the world is, for Sartre, simply the condition for individual moral responsibility, and the source of the moral dignity of the individual person.

This discussion of the role of absurdity should have made clear that, whatever the case for other existentialists, Sartre does not insist upon the absurdity of the world in order to relieve the individual from the responsibility of acting in it or upon it. Science retains its value, as a means toward the realization of individual and social ends. The hostility of the world, as well as its friendliness, is a function of the project of the individual. The Sartrean existentialist could hardly assume the posture of cursing the world for a state of affairs whose existence is the product of his own will. Not, of course, in the sense that as an individual he can control all events, but in the sense that the particular events are bad because he chooses to regard them as such. Sartre himself reacts by proclaiming the total responsibility of the individual for the world in which he lives and by urging him to work toward remedying that which he finds to be evil. If the absurdity of the world as Sartre conceives it is a pessimistic view, it is a pessimism entirely different from the Spenglerian or Schopenhauerian varieties. If the world cannot be considered objectively good, neither can it be considered objectively evil; it is, in effect, what men make of it.

The relative pessimism of Sartrean existentialism lies not in the absurdity of the world as such, but rather, in the first place, in his insistence that anguish is inseparable from action. Freedom, which is the source of man's dignity, is also a source of suffering. This suffering cannot be avoided, for, since man makes the world by his actions, inaction is a form of action. In the second place, Sartre's picture of society can be described as pessimistic because he finds conflict to be a permanent part of interpersonal relations. It is true that, in his social ethics, he finds a partial remedy for this in respect for the freedom of the other. But the differences in power, status, and wealth which characterize societies buttress man's natural inclination to seek an escape from this conflict in bad faith, either by reducing others to an object status or by accepting himself as an object. The search for security which motivates escapism would seem to be a permanent part of the human condition, because the alternative of authenticity and the anguish that goes with it are difficult to bear. Moreover, while reforms in the social structure could make authenticity easier, every child in each generation must progress from a world of ready-made values to the acceptance of responsibility as an individual for his actions. Thus Sartre breaks with the optimism characteristic of the West since the Renaissance, which gave birth to both liberalism and Marxism, and responds to the modern climate of opinion which demands a "pessimistic humanism." He does so without abandoning the call to social reform; instead of the "good society," in which absolute justice is realized, he looks to a better society in which the more serious injustices of this one are remedied. Sartre endeavors to combine a relatively pessimistic assessment of the possibilities of perfection in history with political progressivism.

Catholicism, which shares the view that a perfect society on earth is impossible, is criticized by Sartre because it is a conservatism. The definition of human nature as sinful and subject to moral obligations of supposedly eternal validity gives an artificially static picture of society and tends to justify the status quo. Liberalism, since the middle class has become the dominant social class, serves the same function. Natural rights doctrine serves to provide the prosperous with a moral justification of their privileges, utilitarianism prevents the raising of embarrassing questions by wedding an industrious class to their everyday affairs, and idealism blocks social progress by calling for the integration of the individual into the already existing social system. All three types of liberalism refuse to see society in terms of conflicting classes and power struggles between groups, the actual agents of social change, and are thus conservative in effect. Marxism has the advantage of being the doctrine of a class still seeking reform, in France if not in the Soviet Union, but threatens to become in its turn a conservatism after the "classless society" is achieved. Only existentialism envisages a constant effort toward reform of succeeding imperfect social systems. Insofar as an ideology is characterized by a vision of the good society Sartre's criticisms go beyond the three doctrines which have been described to reject all ideologies. Social reform, in his eyes, should not stem from an attempt to bring society into conformity with a rationally formulated ideal society, but rather from the moral protest of individual citizens against what they feel to be the significant abuses of their time.

Sartre accepts the concept of reason characteristic of modern science, which limits itself to describing reality by hypothetical statements of a greater or lesser degree of predictability and excludes values as not subject to rational determination. He uses it to undermine the supposed rational foundations of all three ideologies. This attitude toward reason is a consequence of the absurdity of the world, and of the fact that it is human subjectivity which brings reason as well as values into the world. Sartre's restriction of reason to what might be termed its technical uses is typical of the existentialist school in philosophy. Reason is seen as a tool whose use is limited to those areas of human experience for which it is by nature suited; for example, it can discover the relationship between means and valued ends, but the definition of these ends is beyond its scope. The values presiding over a project of social reform, therefore, are irrational in origin, the product of an individual-in-situation.

This view of the limitations of reason in social philosophy constitutes a rejection of the rationalist tradition which goes back to Plato and includes Catholicism, liberalism, and pseudoscientific Marxism. Insofar as Sartre holds that the value orientation freely chosen by the individual in the form of his project is prior in importance to reason he can be described as an irrationalist. There are, however, aspects to Sartre's thought which tend to belie this description. He resembles the classical rationalists in that he inveighs against myth as the basis for politics; this is the ground for much of his criticism of the ideologies. To insist that reason be unambiguously confined to the areas in which it has been proved competent, and to accept it as authoritative in these areas, implies a respect for reason unusual in an irrationalist. In addition, Sartre's theory of human reality, although original in its formulation, presents a picture of man which bears a strong resemblance in its parts to the findings of psychology and sociology about human behavior. It is true that Sartre is concerned with human *being*, and not simply prediction of human behavior. He avoids the error of which he accuses the Marxists, that of reading scientific laws as descriptions of reality, and bases his theory on the phenomenological method, which yields knowledge by intuition. This method is currently the subject of much discussion among philosophers, and there is no general agreement as to its validity, but it seems to imply a degree of discipline which falls short of pure irrationalism. Even if one were to suspect that Sartre's intuitions were influenced by his knowledge of sociology, this would merely indicate a possibility that he is the type of old-fashioned rationalist which he accuses the Marxists of being.

It is certainly not without significance that, of all the existentialists, Sartre has provided us with the most systematic and rationally coherent exposition of human reality. As a consequence, he is probably the easiest of approach and most appealing of existentialists for those die-hard rationalists who are dissatisfied with their traditional homes but not ready to make the transition to revelation. There is nothing in Sartre's doctrine which is inconsistent with the scientific study of society, of individual or group behavior. The fact that the ultimate motivation of individual behavior is irrational is not inconsistent with rational analysis of such behavior, any more than the irrationality of atoms would be a bar to the prediction of their movements. Generally speaking, the positivist philosophers are in agreement with Sartre in excluding the determination of ultimate values from the competency of reason, and they would hardly go so far as to deny the importance of such values in human life. Yet they are not ordinarily termed irrationalists. Lastly, Sartre's irrationalism does not require a sacrifice of rationality in the daily life of the individual. He does show how an attempt to repress one's emotions in order to fit oneself into a rationally constructed theory of the good life can be a form of bad faith, but authenticity has its own kind of rationality, which is that of a willingness to learn from experience, to suspend judgment until all the evidence is in, and to suit one's actions to the facts of a situation. Reasoning where the outcome is in doubt is uncongenial to those in bad faith because it threatens to carry them away from the security of their certainties.

A final consequence of the absurdity of the world for Sartre is the comparatively more important role of individual moral responsibility. His philosophical objection to the other doctrines is augmented by criticism in the name of morality: the belief in an ordered universe is an indication of bad faith. Catholicism, liberalism, and Marxism, each in a different way, offer a place to individual moral creativity. Sartre apparently feels that if the individual is offered a system within which to be creative, he will accept the system but neglect to create. So Sartre withdraws the system and tells him that he is morally creative whether he likes it or not, and that he may as well grin and bear it. There is considerable skepticism among commentators whether the average person is sufficient to the task which Sartre sets for him. Whether he is or not, it would seem that Sartre's demands on the individual are required by the time. On the one hand, the modern period is involved not in the realization of universal man but in constant and conscious social change. Sartre speaks approvingly of the United States as being particularly characterized by such change, and the conscious pursuit of social novelty is justified by his philosophy. Social and political change cause moral standards to become outmoded, and the responsibility for the preservation of morality in social relationships is shifted from tradition to individual initiative, since progress in this domain can come only from the initiative of individuals.

On the other hand, it has often enough been observed that things are in the saddle and riding mankind. Whether this results from the materialistic decadence of Western culture, the growth of large-scale organization with its concomitant specialization, or the rapid progress of applied science, its characteristic moral tone has been the loss of individual and group purposes. Sartre makes no effort to resurrect the values of a dead past. Instead, he recalls the individual from "the world of the immediate" or everyday life, and bids him consider his actions in the light of their ultimate moral purposes. This is a direct challenge to the apparent trend of the age toward an "extrovert harmony with the established drift of life" having as its final goal "that human consciousness itself will slowly relax its tension and become dissipated." [2] Sartre offers the individual and the group an open field for the construction of new values, simply insisting that the job get under way.

This restoration to the individual of a central role in

social processes is combined with an insistence upon the importance of the social milieu in determining human nature and as a condition for individual self-realization. Such a combination is, in Sartre's view, the answer to the most pressing problem of modern social philosophy:

. . . the contemporary conscience seems torn apart by an antinomy. Those who hold above all to the dignity of the human person, to his liberty, to his imprescriptible rights, are inclined by this very fact to think according to the spirit of analysis which considers individuals outside of their real conditions of existence, which endows them with an unchanging and abstract human nature. Those who have well understood that man is rooted in the collectivity and who wish to affirm the importance of economic, technical and historical factors rely upon the spirit of synthesis which, blind to persons, only has eyes for groups.[3]

It is as an attempt to provide an escape from this antinomy that Sartre advances his theory of man as freedom-in-situation, totally committed and yet totally free. His position, in this context, would seem to be an effort to bridge the gap between Marxism and liberalism. In order to determine the implications of existentialism for social philosophy it will be useful to summarize the similarities and differences between Sartre's theory and the major themes of the doctrines which he criticizes.

The three elements which seem basic to liberalism are individualism, rationalism, and optimism. Beginning with the first of the three, liberal individualism involves an emphasis on the moral dignity of the individual because of his nature as a free moral agent. He is usually pictured as able to decide freely between alternative courses of action, thus being responsible for his acts. Usually associated with liberal individualism are the doctrine of equality, individual rights as limitations on the state, and the general welfare defined in terms of the welfare of individuals. There is no question but what Sartre shares with the liberals an emphasis on the moral dignity of the individual. However, his view of individual freedom is quite different from the traditional liberal view. Sartre's individual is, in the daily decisions of his life, determined by a prerational choice of himself. All actions, or refusals to act, are a reflection of this initial choice, and the individual is responsible not just for "free" decisions but for his life and world. This concept of freedom as autonomy offers several advantages over the liberal view; it is more consistent with the perspectives of modern psychology, it enables Sartre to avoid the difficulties involved in the classical defense of free will, and it avoids divorcing the reflective and emotional elements in human life. It also offers an intelligible basis for individual equality, all men being equally free in the sense of autonomous, and Sartre is not obliged to assert equality as an addition to his system on the basis of self-evidence, equality before God, or otherwise. It offers, however, an apparent disadvantage, that of abolishing universal values and establishing moral anarchy. Whatever difficulty liberals may have in justifying equality and individual rights, and in deriving a concept of the general welfare which is consistent with their individualism, Sartre's position would seem to exclude any recourse to either individual rights or the general welfare, since they lack any moral sanction but that given to them by the individual.

This raises the question whether Sartre does not push individualism to the point of anarchism or the denial of any moral basis for obedience to authority. This question has already been answered, at least by implication. Sartre does, in fact, reject all constituted systems of

value in favor of the moral creativity of the individual.
At the same time, however, he supplies a new definition
of the social nature of man and a new moral justification
for political organization. His position in both respects is
typically existentialist, and may be summarized here
briefly. Man encounters other persons in his experience;
the content of the experience is the reduction of the self
to the status of an object in the world of the other. This
experience is in itself unpleasant, and in addition establishes the other in a determining position in regard to
the realization of the project, which is the project of a
certain organization of the world. These circumstances
can give rise to conflict, but they can also lead the individual to join with the other in a joint effort to attain
certain social changes which appear to both as desirable.

The principle of respect for the freedom of the other
assumes and goes beyond the initial conflict of individuals. Political action may be a necessary means to social
change, in which case violence is done to the other's
freedom in the name of the greater freedom of all.
Action directed toward the removal of the social barriers
to the freedom of any group promotes the freedom of all.
Man is not free when he is alienated, or unable to give
meaning to his social role in terms of his personal goals.
Conscious pursuit of personal goals is characteristic of
the authentic individual; authenticity cannot be imposed
but it should be allowed self-expression. Personal meaning can be given to one's social role, and alienation
ended, only by the progressive modification of that role
in accordance with personal goals. Political action is
morally justified in placing restrictions upon those members of society whose subjectivity does find expression
in society in order to open up the same possibility to
those who are condemned by society to object status.

Thus Sartre justifies obedience to a political party or a political regime, so long as that regime is or perhaps can become progressive. In like fashion, a claim of individual rights is justified if these rights are politically progressive and not simply a bulwark of the status quo.

The progressive nature of a political program is determined for Sartre by the reality of the values which preside over its formulation. As in the case of his personal ethics, Sartre's social ethics rejects universal values while emphasizing the importance of a value-oriented perspective. The specific personal values of the individual are a function of his project; the social values which he adopts are the condition of the realization of this project for his being-for-others. The affirmation of his being-for-others as valuable is most challenged by those members of the social order to whom he may appear, in virtue of his social function, as an oppressor. His social values are thus determined by the needs of the disinherited, and a political program appears to him as sustained by real values and therefore progressive when it proposes the abolition of socially imposed forms of alienation. These forms are, of course, specific to historical circumstances, and the values of one place and time are strictly relative, although absolute with respect to the particular situation.

Sartre's individualism thus appears to be closer to a reformulation of liberalism than to anarchism. His differences with liberalism are more profound, however, with regard to its rationalism and optimism. Reason is, for liberals of the natural law variety at least, at once a means of access to values and a basic human motivation. In both respects Sartre opposes voluntarism to rationalism; values as well as motives are determined by the choice which the individual makes of himself. It is true that Sartre discerns a suprahistorical human condition, seemingly comparable to the human nature of liberals. This universal condition, however, only sets limits to the variability of human nature. Values, and consequently the political organization of society, are within the realm of the variable. There is, as we have seen, an important element of rationalism in Sartre's philosophy. He joins the liberals in rejecting supernaturalism and holding that a rational grasp of the human condition is the only remedy for those individual and social ills which can be remedied. In comparison with the liberal tradition Sartre can be described as an irrationalist, or as a rationalist willing to admit inconvenient facts inconsistent with earlier rationalism while salvaging what he can of the supremacy of reason. The decision as to which description is the more accurate depends on the attitude of the reader toward the "facts" contained in modern psychoanalytic doctrine, the concept of ideology, and the epistemology of contemporary science.

Finally, Sartre's doctrine presents some stark contrasts with liberal optimism. In the realm of bad faith, social life is conflict. In addition, individual self-realization involves constant striving toward a goal which is, from the beginning, unrealizable. Man is neither good nor bad, but has possibilities for both. Virtue, or what Sartre terms authenticity, offers a partial escape from social conflict, but carries with it anguish rather than happiness. In short, suffering is inevitable, social harmony must be bought at the price of effort and is never fully achieved. Liberal optimism is reduced to the belief that since society is what man makes of it, particular evils can be remedied. Sartre's doctrine can be best described as a pessimistic humanism or, if these two terms seem somewhat contradictory, a very measured optimism.

With respect to Marxism, which shares with the liberals rationalism and optimism, Sartre also appears relatively irrationalistic and pessimistic. Marxist rationalism is naturalistic and opposed to mystification, as is Sartre. Its doctrine of ideology, which makes knowledge and values outgrowths of the life situation of the individual, is close to existentialism, but Marxism makes an exception, in the case of the proletarian, to its doctrine of ideology: the truth of the proletarian is science and his values are of universal validity. At least, this will be true after the proletarian state has reached maturity. Knowledge is for Sartre the outgrowth of experience, which depends upon the intentionality of consciousness as well as upon environmental factors. Science and reason are never pure, but always human. Consequently, Sartre rejects the Marxist laws of history along with the liberal laws of nature. With regard to Marxist optimism, the Sartrean view of the human condition functions primarily as a denial of the historical possibility of the realization of the harmonious society. Marxism itself is more realistic than liberalism; it pictures society as torn by the conflict of classes. Sartre's philosophy justifies this view, broadens it so that class conflict becomes an aspect of interpersonal conflict, and offers with the politics of authenticity only a measured hope, the achievement of particular political reforms. Existentialism is close to Marxism in its view of capitalist societies, but diverges sharply on the subject of the meaning of the construction of socialism.

Two further tendencies of Marxist doctrine are its historicism and its environmentalism. It denies the existence of a universal human nature, regards man as a creature of his historical situation, and views history as a dialectical progression. Sartrean existentialism is in agreement on the subject of human nature, but asserts the permanent reality of the human condition which sets limits to the possibilities of historical change. Also, while the environment determines human nature to a degree, man is to a degree independent of his environment, and determines it in return. In doing so he realizes Marx's dictum that the role of philosophy is to change the world. But, again, the existential utopia is always relative to a given social situation, and never a final solution to the problems of social life. Sartre's refusal to define the individual solely in terms of his environment and his insistence on the relativity of all utopias are of course aspects of his doctrine of freedom. This doctrine of freedom as individual autonomy in its totality is in marked disagreement with the Marxist definition of individual welfare in terms of the good society, and instead retains some of the ambiguities of prerevolutionary society, as described by Marxist analysis, as a part of the permanent condition of man and society.

Finally, Sartrean existentialism can be seen to have a certain congruence with the Christian view of man. Sartre is closer to Niebuhr than to the Catholics on the question of the possibility of a rational understanding of man's essence, but more of a rationalist than either in his naturalism. His voluntarism is closer to some religious views of man than to either liberalism or Marxism, as is his relatively pessimistic view of human perfection which amounts almost to a secular doctrine of original sin. He joins the Christians in placing man's goal beyond history; the fundamental desire to be God relates man as effectively to an ahistorical absolute as the imitation of Christ. The diversity of Christian doctrines makes comparison difficult, but Sartre's essential difference from all Christian views would seem to lie in his rejection of an attitude of faith, or his loyalty to a secular humanism. He makes use of the moral insights of Christianity, and places them within the perspectives of modern social science.

Thus, while Sartre has much in common with the traditional doctrines just discussed, he can hardly be considered a representative of any one of them. He has been rather colorfully described as the Luther to Marx's St. Paul. But his position could be as well described as a reformulation of liberalism or as a secularization of the religious view of man. Of one thing there can be no doubt: he is an existentialist. There are of course many varieties of existentialism, but Sartre hits all the major themes which characterize the philosophy. At the same time, it would be easy to demonstrate that Sartre's philosophy represents a systematization of themes current in French art, literature, and intellectual life which were not inspired by any conscious adherence to existentialist philosophy. To recognize this is only to note that the present success of existentialism is a function of the fact that it satisfies a felt need of the times, and that Sartre's philosophy is a philosophy of and for the twentieth century.

Sartre's message to modern man is to assume his ambiguity. This ambiguity is multiple. Sartre's original definition of man as the being who is not what he is and is what he is not has since been explored and expanded:

1. Man is as he behaves, yet he can never be reduced to what he has done, except when he is dead. As such, he remains fundamentally a mystery.

2. Man is his situation, and cannot be separated from what his place and time have made of him. Yet he is responsible for what he is and for this environment.

3. Man's thought and behavior are determined by his original choice, which is similar to a Freudian determinism in that it is neither rational nor deliberate, and yet he is free.

4. Man's every action is subject to moral interpretation, and yet there are no objective moral principles.

5. Man's fundamental relation with others is conflict, but he can only find himself by committing himself to others.

6. Man and his world have an irrational origin, but salvation lies in the rational recognition of what he is—a sort of reverse stoicism, the living by man of the life determined for him by his project.

Sometimes Sartre emphasizes one facet of the human condition, sometimes another. Since he has never made a systematic presentation of this subject, it is no wonder that many of his interpreters have gone astray. The Marxists accuse him of irrationalism and neglect of social and environmental determination of human nature, the liberals of nihilism, and the Catholics of pessimism. Yet his writings reflect a strong concern with the rational and moral, the possibility of human betterment through social reform, and the impact of exploitation and denial of freedom on the morally responsible individual. In spite of apparent contradictions, Sartre justifies his stand by containing human ambiguity within a coherent theory of man.

NOTES

NOTES TO CHAPTER I

1 Morton White, *The Age of Analysis* (Boston, 1955), p. 18.

2 Søren Kierkegaard, *Concluding Unscientific Post-script*, trans. David F. Swenson and Walter Lowrie (Princeton, 1941), p. 109.

3 *Ibid.*, p. 108.

4 Translated from André Malraux, *Les Noyers de l'Altenburg* (Paris, 1948), pp. 141–42.

5 Emmanuel Mounier, *Introduction aux existentialismes* (Paris, 1947), pp. 2–3.

NOTES TO CHAPTER II

1 Jean-Paul Sartre, *Being and Nothingness*, trans. Hazel Barnes (New York, 1956), p. 621.

2 *Ibid.*, p. 35.

3 Hazel Barnes, Introduction, *ibid.*, p. lxviii.

4 Sartre, *Being and Nothingness*, pp. 262–63.

5 *Ibid.*, p. 410.

6 Iris Murdoch, "Hegel in Modern Dress," *The New Statesman and Nation*, LIII (May 25, 1957), 675.

7 Sartre, *Being and Nothingness*, pp. 239–40.

8 *Ibid.*, p. 3.

NOTES TO CHAPTER III

1 Translated from Jean-Paul Sartre, *La Nausée* (Paris, 1938), p. 238.

2 Jean-Paul Sartre, *Being and Nothingness*, trans. Hazel Barnes (New York, 1956), p. 566.

3   *Ibid.*, pp. 566–67.

4   Alfred Adler, *The Practice and Theory of Individual Psychology* (New York, 1929), p. 3, quoted in Alfred Stern, *Sartre, His Philosophy and Psychoanalysis* (New York, 1953), p. 109.

5   Robert Olson, "The Three Theories of Motivation in the Philosophy of Jean-Paul Sartre," *Ethics*, LXVI, no. 3 (April 1956), 187.

6   Sartre, *Being and Nothingness*, pp. 461–62.

7   *Ibid.*, p. 462.

8   Stern, *op. cit.*, p. 118.

9   Translated from Jean-Paul Sartre, *Saint Genet, comédien et martyr* (Paris, 1952), p. 541.

10 Sartre, *Being and Nothingness*, p. 222.

11 *Ibid.*, p. 262.

12 Translated from Jean-Paul Sartre, "Une Idée fondamentale de Husserl," *Situations*, I (Paris, 1947), 34–35.

13 Sartre, *Saint Genet*, p. 542.

NOTES TO CHAPTER IV

1   Jean-Paul Sartre, *Existentialism*, trans. Bernard Frechtman (New York, 1947), p. 27.

2   *Ibid.*, p. 19.

3   *Ibid.*, pp. 59–60.

4   Marjorie Grene, "Authenticity: an Existentialist Virtue," *Ethics*, LXII, no. 4 (July 1952), 267.

5   Sartre, *Existentialism*, pp. 53–54.

6   Ralph Harper, *Existentialism, a New Theory of Man* (Cambridge, Mass., 1949), p. 103.

7   *Ibid.*, p. 101.

8   Jean-Paul Sartre, *Being and Nothingness*, trans. Hazel Barnes (New York, 1956), p. 556.

9   James Collins, *The Existentialists* (Chicago, 1952), pp. 76–77.

10 Translated from Maurice Merleau-Ponty, *Les Aventures de la dialectique* (Paris, 1955), p. 217.

11 Sartre, *Existentialism*, p. 44.

12 Translated from Jean-Paul Sartre, *Saint Genet, comédien et martyr* (Paris, 1952), p. 547.

13 Sartre, *Existentialism*, p. 54.

14 Translated from Jean-Paul Sartre, "Présentation des temps modernes," *Situations*, II (Paris, 1948), 15.

15 Reinhold Niebuhr, *Christian Realism and Political Problems* (New York, 1953), p. 110.

16 Alfred Stern, *Sartre, His Philosophy and Psychoanalysis* (New York, 1953), pp. 208–9.

NOTES TO CHAPTER V

1 Translated from Jean-Paul Sartre in *Action* (December 29, 1944), quoted in Albert Pasquier, *Les Doctrines sociales en France* (Paris, 1950), p. 152.

2 Jean-Paul Sartre, *Being and Nothingness*, trans. Hazel Barnes (New York, 1956), p. 232.

3 Heinrich A. Rommen, *The Natural Law* (St. Louis, Mo., 1947), p. 170.

4 Sartre, *Being and Nothingness*, p. 566.

5 *Ibid.*, p. 423.

6 *Ibid.*, p. 415.

7 *Ibid.*, p. 49.

8 *Ibid.*, pp. 55–56.

9 *Ibid.*, p. 50.

10 Translated from Charles Baudelaire, *Oeuvres complètes* (Paris, 1951), pp. 1199–1200.

11 Jean-Paul Sartre, *Baudelaire*, trans. Martin Turnell (Norfolk, Conn., 1950), p. 41.

12 *Ibid.*, p. 59.

13 Erich Fromm, *Escape from Freedom* (New York, 1941), pp. 170–71.

14 Sartre, *Baudelaire*, pp. 66–67.

15 Translated from Jean-Paul Sartre, *Le Sursis* (Paris, 1945), pp. 107–8.

16 *Ibid.*, p. 109.

17 *Ibid.*, p. 157.

18 *Ibid.*, p. 320.

19 Translated from Jean-Paul Sartre, *La Mort dans l'âme* (Paris, 1949), p. 82.

20 Translated from Jean-Paul Sartre, "Les Mouches," *Théâtre* (Paris, 1947), pp. 77–78.

21 Sartre, *Existentialism*, p. 34.

NOTES TO CHAPTER VI

1 Jean-Paul Sartre, *Existentialism*, trans. Bernard Frechtman (New York, 1947), p. 18.

2 *Ibid.*, p. 33.

3 Jean-Paul Sartre, "Qu'est-ce que la littérature?" *Situations*, II (Paris, 1948), 305–6.

4 Sartre, *Existentialism*, p. 26.

5 Jacques Maritain, *Existence and the Existent*, English version by Lewis Galantière and Gerald B. Phelan (New York, 1948), pp. 48–49. See also Etienne Gilson, *L'Etre et l'essence* (Paris, 1948), p. 291.

6 Maritain, *op. cit.*, p. 135.

7 James Collins, *The Existentialists* (Chicago, 1952), p. 66.

8 Maritain, *op. cit.*, p. 55.

9 *Ibid.*, p. 9.

10 Reinhold Niebuhr, *Christian Realism and Political Problems* (New York, 1953), pp. 172–73.

11 Paul Tillich, *The Protestant Era*, trans. James Luther Adams (Chicago, 1948), p. 57.

12 Erich Fromm, *The Art of Loving* (New York, 1956), p. 105.

NOTES TO CHAPTER VII

1 John Locke, *Two Treatises of Government*, ed. Thomas I. Cook (New York, 1947), p. xiv.

2 *Ibid.*, p. 123.

3 Translated from Jean-Paul Sartre, "Explication de 'l'étranger'," *Situations*, I (Paris, 1947), 101. Quotation from Albert Camus, *Le Mythe de Sisyphe* (Paris, 1942), p. 35.

4 Translated from Jean-Paul Sartre, "New-York, ville coloniale," *Situations*, III (Paris, 1949), 119–21.

5   Jean-Paul Sartre, *Existentialism,* trans. Bernard Frecht-
    man (New York, 1947), p. 25.

6   Translated from Jean-Paul Sartre, *La Nausée* (Paris,
    1938), p. 155.

7   *Ibid.,* p. 167.

8   *Ibid.,* p. 158.

9   *Ibid.,* p. 175.

10 Translated from Jean-Paul Sartre, "L'Enfance d'un chef,"
    Le Mur (Paris, 1939), p. 243.

11 Richard Hofstadter, "The Pseudo-Conservative Revolt,"
    The New American Right, ed. Daniel Bell (New York,
    1955), pp. 33–55.

12 T. W. Adorno, Else Frenkel-Brunswik, Daniel J. Levin-
    son, and R. Nevitt Sanford, *The Authoritarian Personality*
    (New York, 1950), p. 733.

13 Translated from Sartre, "L'Enfance d'un chef," *op. cit.,*
    p. 243.

14 Translated from Jean-Paul Sartre, "Qu'est-ce que la
    littérature?" *Situations,* II (Paris, 1948), 150–51.

15 *Ibid.,* p. 266.

16 Jeremy Bentham, *A Fragment on Government and an
    Introduction to the Principles of Morals and Legislation,*
    ed. Wilfrid Harrison (New York, 1948), p. 51.

17 Translated from Sartre, "Qu'est-ce que la littérature?"
    op. cit., p. 156.

18 Translated from Jean-Paul Sartre, "Présentation des
    temps modernes," *Situations,* II (Paris, 1948), 17.

19 *Ibid.,* p. 18.

20 *Ibid.,* p. 22.

21 *Ibid.,* pp. 26–27.

22 *Ibid.,* p. 23.

23 Georg Wilhelm Friedrich Hegel, *Reason in History, A
    General Introduction to the Philosophy of History,* trans.
    Robert S. Hartman (New York, 1953), p. 12.

24 *Ibid.,* pp. 15–16.

25 Translated from Sartre, "Qu'est-ce que la littérature?"
    op. cit., p. 158.

26 Jean-Paul Sartre, *Being and Nothingness,* trans. Hazel
    Barnes (New York, 1956), pp. 59–60.

NOTES TO CHAPTER VIII

1   Translated from Jean-Paul Sartre, "Matérialisme et révo-
    lution," *Situations*, III (Paris, 1949), 142–43.
2   *Ibid.*, p. 173.
3   *Ibid.*, pp. 177–78.
4   *Ibid.*, p. 178.
5   Jean-Paul Sartre, *Being and Nothingness*, trans. Hazel
    Barnes (New York, 1956), pp. 434–35.
6   *Ibid.*, pp. 548–49.
7   Translated from Sartre, "Matérialisme et révolution,"
    op. cit., p. 191.
8   *Ibid.*, pp. 210–11.
9   *Ibid.*, p. 162.
10 Sartre, *Being and Nothingness*, p. 580.
11 Translated from Jean-Paul Sartre, "L'Homme et les
    choses," *Situations*, I (Paris, 1947), 288.
12 Translated from Jean-Paul Sartre, *La Mort dans l'âme*
    (Paris, 1949), p. 263.
13 Translated from Jean-Paul Sartre, *Les Mains sales* (Paris,
    1948), pp. 206–8.
14 Sartre, *Being and Nothingness*, p. 580.

NOTES TO CHAPTER IX

1   Jean-Paul Sartre, *Existentialism*, trans. Bernard Frecht-
    man (New York, 1947), p. 87.
2   *Ibid.*, p. 86.
3   *Ibid.*, p. 88.
4   Jean-Paul Sartre, *Being and Nothingness*, trans. Hazel
    Barnes (New York, 1956), p. 364.
5   *Ibid.*, pp. 420–21.
6   Translated from Jean-Paul Sartre, *Saint Genet, comédien
    et martyr* (Paris, 1952), p. 542.
7   Sartre, *Being and Nothingness*, pp. 428–29.
8   *Ibid.*, p. 423.
9   *Ibid.*, p. 424.
10 Translated from Georges Lukacs, *Existentialisme ou
    Marxisme?* (Paris, 1948), pp. 146–47.

11   *Ibid.*, p. 286.

12   *Ibid.*, p. 188.

13   Herbert Read, *Existentialism, Marxism and Anarchism* (London, 1950), p. 10.

14   Translated from Lukacs, *op. cit.*, p. 98.

15   *Ibid.*, p. 28.

NOTES TO CHAPTER X

1   Translated from Albert Pasquier, *Les Doctrines sociales en France 1930–1950* (Paris, 1950), p. 174.

2   Translated from Jean-Paul Sartre, "La Liberté cartésienne," *Situations*, I (Paris, 1947), 332–33.

3   *Ibid.*, p. 334.

4   *Ibid.*, p. 330.

5   Translated from Descartes, *Traité des passions*, art. 153, quoted in *Ibid.*, pp. 329–30.

6   *Ibid.*, p. 319.

7   Eric Voegelin, *The New Science of Politics* (Chicago, 1952), p. 163.

8   Henri Magnan, ". . . Said Jean-Paul Sartre," *Yale French Studies*, XVI (Winter 1955–56), 5.

NOTES TO CHAPTER XI

1   Ernst Topitsch, "The Sociology of Existentialism," *Partisan Review*, XXI, no. 3 (May–June 1954), 298.

2   Roderick Seidenberg, *Post-historic Man* (Chapel Hill, N.C., 1950), pp. 187–88.

3   Translated from Jean-Paul Sartre, "Présentation des temps modernes," *Situations*, II (Paris, 1948), 222–23.